Grammar
Review

Printed in the U.S.A.

ISBN 978-0-544-26183-9

1 2 3 4 5 6 7 8 9 10   0982   22 21 20 19 18 17 16 15 14

4500460777   A B C D E F G

Core Skills Grammar Review

Table of Contents

© Houghton Mifflin Harcourt Publishing Company

* Aligns to the English Language Arts Common Core
State Standards.

© Houghton Mifflin Harcourt Publishing Company

Introduction

Core Skills Grammar Review was developed to help students improve the language skills they need to succeed. The book emphasizes skills in the following key areas.

- grammar
- punctuation
- vocabulary
- spelling

The lessons included in the book provide many opportunities for students to practice and apply important grammar and mechanics skills. These skills will help each student excel in all academic areas, increase his or her scores on standardized tests, and have a greater opportunity for success in his or her career.

About the Book

The book is divided into four units:

- Vocabulary
- Sentences
- Grammar and Usage
- Capitalization, Punctuation, and Spelling

Students can work through each unit of the book, or you can pinpoint areas that need extra practice.

Lessons have specific instructions and examples and are designed for students to complete independently. Grammar lessons range from using nouns and verbs to constructing better sentences. With this practice, students will gain extra confidence as they work on daily school lessons or standardized tests.

A thorough answer key is also provided to check the quality of answers.

A Step Toward Success

Practice may not always make perfect, but it is certainly a step in the right direction. The activities in *Core Skills Grammar Review* are an excellent way to ensure greater success for every student.

Check What You Know

Write H before each pair of homonyms, S before each pair of synonyms, and A before each pair of antonyms.

_____ **1.** board, bored

_____ **2.** tall, short

_____ **3.** antique, ancient

_____ **4.** massive, huge

Write the homograph for the pair of meanings.

_____ **5.** a piece of hair; to fasten securely

Write P before each word with a prefix, S before each word with a suffix, and C before each compound word.

_____ **6.** diagram

_____ **7.** misplace

_____ **8.** surfboard

_____ **9.** variance

_____ **10.** rusty

_____ **11.** nightstand

Underline the word in parentheses that has the more negative connotation.

12. The (crabby, unhappy) child squirmed in her mother's arms.

Underline the more precise word in parentheses.

13. It was a (nice, sunny) day.

14. Sit in the (chair, recliner).

Circle the number of the idiom that means to suddenly become angry.

15. put up with

16. fly off the handle

Underline the figurative language in each sentence.

17. We've been down this road a million times.

18. The mountains opened their arms and hugged the hikers.

Write D before the declarative sentence, IM before the imperative sentence, E before the exclamatory sentence, and IN before the interrogative sentence. Then underline the simple subject and circle the simple predicate in each sentence.

_____ **19.** Wait until the speech is over.

_____ **20.** What do you believe?

_____ **21.** Ouch! I burned myself!

_____ **22.** That article really made me angry.

Write CS before the sentence that has a compound subject and CP before the sentence that has a compound predicate.

_____ **23.** He stumbled and fell on the rough ground.

_____ **24.** Carmen and Jose are the leading actors.

Write CS before the compound sentence. Write RO before the run-on sentence. Write F before the sentence fragment.

_____ **25.** Drove all the way to the orchard to buy apples.

_____ **26.** Once she had lived in New York, she lives in Toronto now.

_____ **27.** Brenda was cold, so she built a roaring fire.

1

Put brackets around each dependent clause and underline each independent clause. Write <u>CX</u> before the complex sentence and <u>CD-CX</u> before the compound-complex sentence.

_____ **28.** After I moved into town, I rented a beautiful new apartment.

_____ **29.** Jill was right on time, and she smiled when she arrived.

Underline the common nouns and circle the proper nouns in the sentence.

30. Ms. Chang rounded up the group and began the tour of the Jefferson Memorial.

Circle the appositive in the sentence. Underline the noun it identifies or explains.

31. My favorite uncle, Tom Fiske, was recently elected mayor of Greenville.

Write <u>past</u>, <u>present</u>, or <u>future</u> to show the tense of each underlined verb.

32. _____ Kathy <u>painted</u> one wall in her kitchen pale blue.

33. _____ Peter <u>will call</u> at about eight o'clock tonight.

34. _____ Each morning before breakfast, Juan <u>walks</u> two miles.

Underline the participial phrase and circle the infinitive phrase.

35. Waiting to go on stage, Derek started to feel nervous.

Circle the number of the sentence that is in the active voice.

36. The packages were sent two weeks ago.

37. Phillip leaped to his feet to disagree with the speaker.

Underline the correct verb in each sentence.

38. Where (is, are) the balloons for the party?

39. Each of the boys (enjoys, enjoy) soccer.

40. The sprouts on this salad (tastes, taste) delicious.

Write <u>SP</u> before the sentence that has a subjective pronoun, <u>OP</u> before the sentence that has an objective pronoun, <u>PP</u> before the sentence that has a possessive pronoun, and <u>IP</u> before the sentence that has an indefinite pronoun. Circle the pronoun in each sentence.

_____ **41.** Nobody understands what happened.

_____ **42.** Ellen played the first song for him.

_____ **43.** The horse raised its head to look at the dog.

_____ **44.** He sent the memo to four people.

Underline the pronoun. Circle its antecedent.

45. Janet and Jason met to discuss the response to their request.

Write <u>adjective</u> or <u>adverb</u> to describe the underlined word.

46. _____ <u>These</u> days are the best of the summer.

47. _____ Charlotte tiptoed <u>quietly</u> past the open door.

48. _____ I really like <u>Canadian</u> bacon on my pizza.

49. _____ The dachshund is a <u>tiny</u> breed of dog.

2

Check What You Know
Core Skills Grammar Review

50. _____ That <u>heavy</u> tree will be extremely hard to move.

Underline each prepositional phrase twice. Circle each preposition. Underline the conjunction once.

51. I don't have the time or the patience to talk about the complaints of those people.

Circle the number of the sentence that is written correctly.

52. Leaping across the stage, we were amazed by the dancer's performance.

53. Leaping across the stage, the dancer amazed us with her performance.

Underline the correct word in parentheses.

54. The kitten (could, couldn't) barely walk.

55. Don't make (any, no) more promises.

56. That hamster is the (cutest, most cutest) thing I've ever seen.

57. Rewrite the email below. Add capital letters and punctuation where needed.

hello steve,

well I wanted to check in with you_____ how was your week at the lake with milly and the girls_____ we had such a good time visiting aunt amy_____ you wont believe what no I'll wait until I see you to tell you that story_____ lets just say that her other guests who were quite adventurous led us into some interesting situations_____ we were fortunate to have mild sunny weather most days_____ the drive back just three hours on the open road with very little traffic was even fairly pleasant_____

were so excited youre coming to visit_____ even little jason managed to say uncle steve visit which was pretty good for a child of only twenty two months_____ wouldnt you agree_____ harriet mills our next door neighbor is looking forward to meeting you by the way_____

oh I want to be sure I have the information correct_____ please let me know as soon as possible if any of this is wrong flight 561 310 P.M. may 22_____ see you then_____

amanda

_____

_____

_____

_____

_____

_____

_____

Underline the correctly spelled word in each pair.

58. receipt, reciept

59. usualy, usually

60. peice, piece

61. loveliest, lovelyest

62. trimer, trimmer

63. cryed, cried

Check What You Know Correlation Chart

Below is a list of the sections on *Check What You Know* and the pages on which the skills in each section are taught. If you missed any questions, turn to the pages listed and practice the skills. Then correct the problems you missed on *Check What You Know*.

Items	Skill	Practice Page
1-4	Homonyms	5
1-4	Synonyms and Antonyms	14
5	Homographs	6
6-11	Compound Words	7
6-11	Prefixes	10-11
6-11	Suffixes	12-13
12	Connotation and Denotation	18
12-14	Word Choice	19
15-16	Idioms	20
17-18	Figurative Language	21-23
19-22	Types of Sentences	30
23-24	Simple Subjects and Predicates	31
23-24	Compound Subjects	34
23-24	Compound Predicates	35
25-29	Compound and Complex Sentences	39-40
25-27	Correcting Fragments	42
25-29	Correcting Run-on Sentences	43
28-29	Independent and Dependent Clauses	37
28-29	Compound-Complex Sentences	41
30	Common and Proper Nouns	52
31	Appositives	58
32-34	Verb Tenses	60-61
35	Infinitives and Infinitive Phrases	64
35	Participles and Participial Phrases	65

Items	Skill	Practice Page
36-37	Active and Passive Voice	70
38-40	Subject-Verb Agreement	72-73
41-45	Pronouns	74
41-44	Demonstrative, Indefinite, and Intensive Pronouns	75
45	Antecedents	76
46-50	Adjectives	80
46-50	Demonstrative Adjectives	81
46-50	Adverbs	83
46-50	Adjectives and Adverbs	85
51	Prepositions	86
51	Prepositional Phrases	87
51	Conjunctions	90
52-53	Misplaced and Dangling Modifiers	89
54-56	Nonstandard Usage	91
57	Capitalization	96-97
57	End Punctuation	98
57	Commas	99-102
57	Quotation Marks and Apostrophes	103
57	Hyphens, Colons, and Semicolons	104
57	Parentheses, Dashes, and Ellipses	105
58-63	Spelling	106-107

Homonyms

A **homonym** is a word that sounds the same as another word but has a different spelling and a different meaning.

Example: their — they're — there   hear — here

Underline the correct homonym(s) in each sentence below.

1. What is the (weight, wait) of that rocket?
2. The (sale, sail) on the lake will be rough today.
3. Don't you like to (brows, browse) around in a bookstore?
4. We spent several (days, daze) at an old-fashioned (in, inn).
5. The ship was caught in an ice (flow, floe).
6. A large (boulder, bolder) rolled down the mountainside.
7. Why is that crowd on the (pier, peer)?
8. They asked the bank for a (lone, loan).
9. We drove four miles in a foggy (missed, mist).
10. Don't you like to (sea, see) a field of golden wheat?
11. Jack (threw, through) the ball (threw, through) the garage window.
12. We (buy, by) our fish from the market down on the (beach, beech).
13. The band will march down the middle (aisle, isle) of the auditorium.
14. Who is the (principal, principle) of your school?
15. The United States Congress (meals, meets) in the Capitol in Washington, D.C.
16. The farmer caught the horse by the (rain, reign, rein).
17. She stepped on the (break, brake) suddenly.
18. (Their, There) are too many people to get on this boat.
19. The wren (flew, flue) in a (strait, straight) line.
20. We were not (allowed, aloud) to visit the museum yesterday.

Write a homonym for each word below.

21. weigh _____
22. steal _____
23. sail _____
24. fare _____
25. maid _____
26. deer _____

27. ate _____
28. vain _____
29. strait _____
30. threw _____
31. soar _____
32. bored _____

33. see _____
34. sent _____
35. pare _____
36. peace _____
37. sun _____
38. blue _____

5

Unit 1: Vocabulary
Core Skills Grammar Review

Homographs

> A **homograph** is a word that has the same spelling as another word but a different meaning and sometimes a different pronunciation.
>
> **Example:** <u>saw</u>, meaning "have seen," and <u>saw</u>, meaning "a tool used for cutting"

Circle the letter for the definition that best defines each underlined homograph.

1. Sara jumped at the <u>bangs</u> of the exploding balloons.

   a. fringe of hair   **b.** loud noises

2. She grabbed a stick to <u>arm</u> herself against the threat.

   a. part of the body   **b.** take up a weapon

3. Rover's loud <u>bark</u> woke the whole family.

   a. noise a dog makes   **b.** outside covering on a tree

4. Mix the pancake <u>batter</u> for three minutes.

   a. person at bat   **b.** mixture for cooking

Use the homographs in the box to complete the sentences below. Each homograph will be used twice.

```
duck
alight
can
checkers
```

5. Pieces of a board game are _____.

   People who are cashiers are _____.

6. A _____ is a kind of water bird.

   To lower the head is to _____.

7. A metal container is a _____.

   If you are able, you _____.

8. To get down from something is to _____.

   If something is on fire, it is _____.

Write the homograph for each pair of meanings below. The first letter of each word is given for you.

9. **a.** place for horses   **b.** delay   s _____

10. **a.** a metal fastener   **b.** a sound made with fingers   s _____

11. **a.** to crush   **b.** a yellow vegetable   s _____

12. **a.** a bad doctor   **b.** the sound made by a duck   q _____

13. **a.** to strike   **b.** a party fruit drink   p _____

Compound Words

A **compound word** is a word that is made up of two or more words. The meaning of many compound words is related to the meaning of each individual word.

Example: blue + berry = blueberry, meaning "a type of berry that is blue in color"

Compound words may be written as one word, as a hyphenated word, or as two separate words. Always check a dictionary.

Combine the words in the list to make compound words. You may use words more than once.

air	knob	door	port	paper	condition	black	berry
sand	line	stand	under	way	ground	bird	sea

1. _____   7. _____

2. _____   8. _____

3. _____   9. _____

4. _____   10. _____

5. _____   11. _____

6. _____   12. _____

Answer the following questions.

13. Whirl means "to move in circles." What is a whirlpool?

_____

14. Since quick means "moves rapidly," what is quicksand?

_____

15. Rattle means "to make sharp, short sounds quickly." What is a rattlesnake?

_____

16. A ring is "a small circular band." What is an earring?

_____

17. Pool can mean "a group of people who do something together." What is a car pool?

_____

18. A lace can be "a string or cord that is used to hold something together." What is a shoelace?

_____

Roots

The **root** of a word is the part that carries the word's core meaning. Many words in English come from ancient Greek roots.

Example: The word biography, meaning "a written history of a person's life," comes from the Greek roots bios, meaning "life," and graphein, meaning "to write."

Knowing the meanings of some common Greek roots can help you figure out the meanings of new or unfamiliar words.

Greek Root	Meaning
bios	life
chronos	time
graphein	to write
hydra	water
metron	measure
tele	far away
skopein	look at

Write the word from the box that matches the meaning given. Use the chart above and a dictionary if you need it.

autograph	biology	biosphere	cartography	chronology
chronometer	geography	hydrant	hydrate	microscope
speedometer	telescope	telegraph	teleconference	hydroelectric

1. something you can use to write to people far away _____

2. device for measuring speed _____

3. structure to get water for putting out fires _____

4. equipment for looking at something very far away _____

5. sequence of events over time _____

6. study of living things _____

7. drawing maps with written labels of places _____

8. equipment for looking at very small things _____

9. fill with water _____

10. writing of one's own name _____

11. machine for measuring time very accurately _____

12. special environment set up to support life _____

13. meeting held with participants far away from one another _____

14. powered by water _____

15. written information about places on Earth _____

© Houghton Mifflin Harcourt Publishing Company

Unit 1: Vocabulary
Core Skills Grammar Review

Many words in English come from ancient Latin roots.

Example: The Latin root <u>cap</u>, meaning "head," is used to form the English words <u>captain</u>, meaning "head of the ship," and <u>capital</u>, meaning "head of government."

Knowing the meanings of some common Latin roots can help you figure out the meanings of new or unfamiliar words.

Latin Root	Meaning
aqu	water
cent	hundred
dict	say or write
man	hand
mot	move
prim	first, early
spec	look or see

Write the word from the box that matches the meaning given. Use the chart above and a dictionary if you need it.

aquarium	aquifer	century	centimeter	dictionary
dictation	manual	motivate	manage	primary
primitive	manuscript	remote	spectacle	spectator

16. a metric unit of measurement _____

17. to handle with skill _____

18. a glass tank for animals that live in water _____

19. moved far away from _____

20. belonging to the first humans _____

21. a document that is written by hand or typed _____

22. a period of one hundred years _____

23. writing down words that were said _____

24. an area of rock that holds water _____

25. to cause to want to move or change _____

26. an interesting sight to see _____

27. having to do with the main or first one _____

28. worked or done by hand _____

29. someone who sees or watches _____

30. book with list of words from a language _____

Prefixes

A **prefix** added to the beginning of a root word changes the meaning of the word.

> **Example:** <u>un-</u>, meaning "not," + the root word <u>done</u> = <u>undone</u>, meaning "not done"

Some prefixes have one meaning, and others have more than one meaning.

Prefix	Meaning
im-, in-, non-, un-	not
dis-, in-, non-	opposite of, lack of, not
mis-	bad, badly, wrong, wrongly
pre-	before
re-	again

Add the prefix <u>un-</u>, <u>im-</u>, <u>non-</u>, or <u>mis-</u> to the root word in parentheses. Write the new word in the sentence. Then write the definition of the new word on the line after the sentence. Use a dictionary if necessary.

1. It is _____ to put a new monkey into a cage with other monkeys. (practical)

_____

2. The monkeys might _____ with a newcomer among them. (behave)

_____

3. They will also feel quite _____ for a number of days or even weeks. (easy)

_____

4. Even if the new monkey is _____ in nature, the others may harm it. (violent)

_____

5. Sometimes animal behavior can be quite _____. (usual)

_____

Underline each prefix. Write the meaning of each word that has a prefix.

6. unexpected guest _____

7. really disappear _____

8. disagree often _____

9. misspell a name _____

10. preview a movie _____

11. reenter a room _____

12. misplace a shoe _____

Name _____ Date _____

Many common prefixes come from Latin or Greek origins.

Prefix	Origin	Meaning
anti-	Greek	against, opposing
dia-	Greek	through, across, between
hyper-	Greek	excessive, over
de-	Latin	away from, off, down
inter-	Latin	between, among
sub-	Latin	under, beneath

Knowing the meaning of a Greek or Latin prefix can help you figure out the meaning of a word in which it appears.

Example: <u>anti</u>-, meaning "against," + the root word <u>lock</u> = <u>antilock</u>, meaning "keeping from locking"

Underline the prefix in each word. Then guess the meaning of the word and write it on the line. Check your guesses in a dictionary.

13. dialogue _____

14. detach _____

15. subterranean _____

16. antibacterial _____

17. diameter _____

18. interaction _____

19. submarine _____

Add the prefix to the root word shown in parentheses, and write the new word in the sentence. Then write the definition of the new word on the line after the sentence. Use a dictionary if necessary.

20. Your idea is interesting, but I would also like to explore its _____. (anti- + thesis)

_____

21. She actually started to _____ because she was so panicked. (hyper- + ventilate)

_____

22. When riding your bike down a hill, remember to _____ around the turns. (de- + celerate)

_____

23. The builders used _____ materials in that office building. (sub- + standard)

_____

24. Our dog and our guinea pig have developed a special _____ friendship. (inter- + species)

_____

Suffixes

A **suffix** added to the end of a root word changes the meaning of the word. It also changes the word's part of speech.

Example: the root word <u>joy</u> (noun) + <u>-ful</u>, meaning "full of," = <u>joyful</u> (adjective), meaning "full of joy"

Some suffixes have one meaning, and others have more than one meaning.

Suffix	Meaning
-able	able to be, suitable or inclined to
-al	relating to, like
-ful	as much as will fill, full of
-less	without, that does not
-ous	full of
-y	having, full of

Add a suffix from the list above to the root word in parentheses. Write the new word. Then write the definition of the new word on the line after the sentence. Do not use any suffix more than once.

1. Switzerland is a _____ country. (mountain)

_____

2. If you visit there, it is _____ to have a walking stick. (help)

_____

3. Many tourists visit the country's _____ mountains to ski each year. (snow)

_____

4. The Swiss people have a great deal of _____ pride. (nation)

_____

5. Many Swiss are _____ about several languages. (knowledge)

_____

Underline each suffix. Write the meaning of each word that has a suffix.

6. breakable toy _____

7. endless waves _____

8. hazardous path _____

9. inflatable raft _____

10. poisonous snake _____

11. dependable trains _____

12. humorous program _____

Many common suffixes come from Greek and Latin origins.

Suffix	Meaning	Forms a(n)
-ance (Latin)	act, quality	noun
-ible (Latin)	able, likely	adjective
-ic (Greek and Latin)	showing the quality of	adjective
-ize (Greek and Latin)	make, cause	verb
-ment (Latin)	result, act of, state of being	noun
-tude (Latin)	quality, state	noun

Knowing the meaning of a Greek or Latin suffix can help you figure out the meaning of a word in which it appears.

Example: the root word <u>science</u>, meaning "knowledge of nature" + <u>-ic</u>, meaning "showing the quality of" = <u>scientific</u>, meaning "showing the quality of having knowledge of nature"

Underline the suffix in each word. Then guess the meaning of the word and write it on the line. Check your guesses in a dictionary.

13. statement _____

14. socialize _____

15. admittance _____

16. gratitude _____

17. angelic _____

18. brilliance _____

19. visible _____

Add the suffix to the root word shown in parentheses, and write the new word in the sentence. Then write the definition of the new word on the line after the sentence. Use a dictionary if necessary.

20. The photo shows lava coming from the _____ eruption. (volcano + -ic)

_____

21. Do not _____ without also making a positive suggestion. (critic + -ize)

_____

22. Her voice was barely _____ over the noise of the crowd. (audio + -ible)

_____

23. Even the slightest _____ could wake the baby. (move + -ment)

_____

24. The stretching routine helps the athletes stay _____. (flex + -ible)

_____

13

Synonyms and Antonyms

A **synonym** is a word that has the same or nearly the same meaning as one or more other words.

Examples: reply — answer   talk — speak

Write a synonym for each word below.

1. pleasant _____   5. fearless _____   9. house _____

2. enough _____   6. artificial _____   10. nation _____

3. leave _____   7. famous _____   11. difficult _____

4. inquire _____   8. trade _____   12. vacant _____

Write four sentences about recycling. In each sentence, use a synonym for the word in parentheses. Underline the synonym.

13. (packaging) _____

14. (waste) _____

15. (landfill) _____

16. (planet) _____

An **antonym** is a word that has the opposite meaning of another word.

Examples: old — new   bad — good

Write an antonym for each word below.

17. failure _____   21. all _____   25. friend _____

18. absent _____   22. near _____   26. always _____

19. before _____   23. love _____   27. light _____

20. slow _____   24. no _____   28. forward _____

In each sentence, write an antonym for the word in parentheses that makes sense in the sentence.

29. Thao ran his hand along the _____ surface of the wood. (smooth)

30. He knew he would have to _____ sanding it. (stop)

31. Only after sanding would he be able to _____ a table. (destroy)

32. He would try to _____ not to sand it too much. (forget)

Context Clues

The **context** of a word consists of the words, phrases, and sentences that surround it. Often you can figure out the meanings of unfamiliar words by using **context clues**. You can also use context to check the meaning of a word you think you know. Three common types of context clues are **definitions or restatements, examples,** and **synonyms**.

Examples:

Many of our food crops are **hybrids**, <u>combinations of more than one family of plants</u>. (definition)

Advertising, <u>such as TV commercials and billboards</u>, is not always truthful. (examples)

I always suspected he was an **imposter**, and now everyone knows he is a <u>faker</u>. (synonym)

When you guess a word's meaning using context, use a dictionary to check your guess.

Underline the context clues for the underlined word.

1. Armando hopes to one day become an <u>architect</u>, someone who designs buildings.
2. Most <u>citrus</u> trees, including lime trees, orange trees, and lemon trees, thrive in semitropical climates.
3. The amount of <u>arable</u> land—that is, land that can be farmed—is very small in that region.
4. At first I enjoyed the newness of the online game, but the <u>novelty</u> wore off, and I became bored.
5. We wanted to plant a row of <u>conifers</u>—either pine trees or blue spruce—behind the community center.
6. Darlene was angry, and her friend Eduardo was equally <u>incensed</u>.
7. Mr. Yates was so nervous and confused that he upset his co-workers with his <u>distraught</u> behavior.
8. Use <u>concise</u> language in order to make your point in fewer words and less time.
9. When I am sick for more than a few days, I tend to become <u>irritable</u>, or cranky.
10. Fleas, ticks, and other <u>parasites</u> can make your pets miserable.

For each underlined word, write a short definition based on the context clues. Check your definitions in a dictionary.

11. The speaker made an <u>eloquent</u> appeal, using the perfect words to make us want to help.

_____

12. Potters, weavers, and other <u>artisans</u> donated their products to the crafts fair.

_____

13. Emily stayed home because she was <u>infirm</u>, but she still felt sick and rundown the next day.

_____

14. The cafe has <u>amenities</u> such as soft chairs, bookshelves, and wireless Internet access.

_____

15. The judge seemed <u>impartial</u>, not favoring one side in the case over the other.

_____

15

Three other types of context clues are **comparisons**, **contrasts**, and **cause and effect**.

Examples:

The **hawser** is often stronger than all the other ropes on the ship. (comparison)

His **tranquil** expression gave no sign of the panic he was feeling. (contrast)

The temperature rose so high that we were soon **sweltering** even in the shade. (cause and effect)

Underline the context clues for the underlined word.

16. Terriers are often more energetic and willful than other types of dogs.

17. The rash inflamed the baby's skin, so his father soothed it with lotion.

18. Reuben was a meticulous dresser, but his room was not very neat.

19. The performance of a song may be transitory, but the melody can last in a person's memory for a long time.

20. The problem has become apparent; however, the solution remains hidden.

21. Since the disease was spread easily, people who were affected had to be quarantined.

22. Because the saxophone approximates the human voice, it often replaces the singer in jazz compositions.

23. The rebel was once banished from her home, but she was later welcomed back and praised for her courage.

24. I think manicotti, which is larger than most other kinds of pasta, is difficult to cook properly.

25. African Americans brought many different styles of music from Africa and therefore greatly influenced American music.

For each underlined word, write a short definition based on the context clues. Check your definitions in a dictionary.

26. If the violin sounds abrasive, the person playing it may be a beginner.

_____

27. On the tennis court, Ellie and Mei are adversaries, but off the court they are friends.

_____

28. The humble bungalow was much smaller than the mansion where she'd lived as a child.

_____

29. The witness's story was believable; the reporter's explanation, however, seemed dubious.

_____

30. Because Uncle Bert had heart problems, he saw a cardiologist often.

_____

Reference Materials

A **dictionary** entry gives the pronunciation, part of speech, origins, and all the definitions of a word.

Example: li brar y (lī' brer ē) *n., pl.* **li brar ies** [ME *librarie* < OFr *libraire*, person who transcribes books < *liber*, a book] **1** a collection of books, magazines, newspapers, and other materials, especially when arranged and catalogued for public use. **2** a building, room, or other place in which such a collection is kept.

Dictionaries can be in print or online. The words are listed in alphabetical order. Use a dictionary to check meaning, pronunciation, or etymology of an unfamiliar word.

A **glossary** lists the important or difficult words used in a textbook. A glossary entry will only include the meaning of the word as it is used in the book.

Examples: composition The way that forms, colors, and lines are arranged in a given artwork.
cupula A rounded or dome-shaped roof or ceiling.

A **thesaurus** lists the synonyms and antonyms of words. Use a thesaurus to find a word with just the right shade of meaning.

Example: permeate *v.* penetrate, pass through, seep through; pervade, saturate, imbue. --ANT. bounce off, ricochet, glance off.

Use the dictionary entries to answer the questions.

bear[1] (ber) *vt.* [ME *beren* < OE *beran* < IE base *bher* to carry, bring L *ferre*] **1** to carry along. **2** to have or show. **3** to give birth to. **4** to bring forth or produce. **5** to support or hold up.
bear[2] (ber) *n.* [ME *bear* < OE *bera* < IE *bheros*, brown animal] **1** large carnivore with shaggy fur and short tail that walks flat on the soles of its feet. **2** a rude or gruff person.
cam pus (kam' pus) *n.* [L *campus*, field] the grounds and buildings of a school or university.
gar de nia (gar dē' nyə) *n.* [ML Gardenia, from Alexander *Garden*, 1730–1791, U.S. scientist who studied plants] a fragrant yellow or white flower from an evergreen shrub or tree.
ut ter (ət' ər) *v.* [ME or D, *utteren*, literally, out] to express; make known; put forth.

1. Which word comes from a Latin word with the same spelling? _____
2. What part of speech is the word utter? _____
3. What does the Indo-European base word bher mean? _____
4. Which word comes from a person's name? _____
5. What part of speech is the word campus? _____
6. What does the Middle English word utteren mean? _____
7. Which definition of the verb bear fits this sentence: "The lemon tree in the backyard will soon bear fruit"? _____
8. Which definition of the verb bear fits this sentence: "That table is not strong enough to bear a person's weight"? _____

17

Unit 1: Vocabulary
Core Skills Grammar Review

Connotation and Denotation

The **denotation** of a word is its exact meaning as stated in a dictionary.

> **Example:** The denotation of <u>casual</u> is "not fancy or formal."

The **connotation** of a word is an added meaning that suggests something positive or negative.

> **Examples: Negative**: <u>Sloppy</u> suggests "very messy." <u>Sloppy</u> has a negative connotation.
>
> **Positive**: <u>Casual</u> suggests "informal or relaxed." <u>Casual</u> has a positive connotation.

Some words are neutral. They do not suggest either good or bad feelings.

> **Examples:** calendar, toy, pencil

Write (−) if the word has a negative connotation. Write (+) if it has a positive connotation. Write (N) if the word is neutral.

1. _____ lazy
   _____ relaxed

2. _____ determined
   _____ stubborn

3. _____ stingy
   _____ economical

4. _____ clever
   _____ sneaky

5. _____ pretty
   _____ gorgeous

6. _____ grand
   _____ large

7. _____ old
   _____ antique

8. _____ curious
   _____ nosy

9. _____ make
   _____ create

10. _____ weird
    _____ unique

11. _____ criticize
    _____ evaluate

12. _____ snooty
    _____ refined

Rewrite the paragraph below. Replace the underlined words with words that do not have a negative connotation.

Jason <u>shoved</u> his way through the <u>mob</u> of people. He <u>swaggered</u> through the doorway and <u>slouched</u> against the wall. His clothes were quite <u>gaudy</u>. He <u>glared</u> at everyone with <u>hostile</u> eyes. Then he <u>snickered</u> and said in a <u>loud</u> tone, "I'm finally here."

_____

_____

_____

_____

_____

Word Choice

Choose precise, vivid words instead of vague ones to improve your writing.

Precise words are specific words that make a description or explanation exact, sharp, and clear.
Vivid language makes writing seem fresher and more interesting.

    Example: The puppy ran down the street. (flat and boring)
The clumsy little puppy went bounding down the street, tumbling every few feet. (vivid and exciting)

Underline the more precise or vivid word choice in parentheses.

1. That roller coaster ride was so (fun, thrilling).

2. I had a (nice, fantastic) time at the (picnic, event).

3. We were soothed by the (cool, rhythmic) sounds of our footsteps as we hiked.

4. June was (surprised, startled) by a loud (clatter, noise) in the other room.

5. The players (drank, gulped) their sports drinks during the break.

6. Lily was drawn to that college because of its (sprawling, large) campus.

7. The fog was (bad, dense) in the valley.

8. Suddenly the (thin, spindly) woman (turned, spun) toward me and began shouting.

9. That rock formation (is cool looking, looks like a giant bear's head).

10. This house is almost too (big, spacious) for one person.

11. I could hardly stand to see the (devastated, sad) look on the toddler's face.

12. We sat (a long time, for hours) looking at the (beautiful, snowcapped) mountains.

13. Mother's (look, gaze) can be (scary, bone chilling) when she is disappointed in us.

14. Our (stroll, walk) in the (wildflower field, meadow) was (nice, delightful).

15. (Dark, Jet-black) smoke rose from the spot of the explosion.

Rewrite each sentence, adding details and using vivid, precise language.

16. The class is difficult.

_____

17. The shop had lots of nice things.

_____

18. Our drive across the state was unpleasant.

_____

19. The kitten looks cute when she is sleeping.

_____

20. The customer slowly walked out, speaking quietly to herself.

_____

Idioms

An **idiom** is an expression that has a meaning different from the usual meanings of the individual words within it.

Example: We're all in the same boat means "We're in a similar situation," not "We're all in a watercraft together."

Read each sentence. Then write the letter of the corresponding idiom for the underlined word or words.

A. shaken up	**D.** beside herself	**G.** comes through	**J.** down in the dumps
B. fly off the handle	**E.** in a bind	**H.** in the doghouse	**K.** stands up for
C. on cloud nine	**F.** put up with	**I.** on the fence	

1. One day Julia will be <u>sad</u>. __A__

2. The next day you may find her <u>unbelievably happy</u>. __C__

3. But be careful when Julia is <u>very scared or confused</u>. __E__

4. She's liable to <u>become suddenly angry</u>. __B__

5. Julia always <u>defends</u> her views, no matter what. __K__

6. She won't <u>allow</u> any argument. __F__

7. One time when I insisted that she listen to my viewpoint, she was <u>really upset</u>. __D__

8. I was <u>out of favor</u> for weeks. __J__

9. On the other hand, when a friend of Julia's is <u>in a difficult situation</u>, she really <u>helps</u>. __H__ __G__

10. Like a true friend, Julia is there when I am <u>unable to make a decision</u>. __I__

For the underlined idiom in each sentence below, write the usual meaning of the words that make up the idiom.

11. Kelly can't decide whether she wants to go, so our plans are still <u>up in the air</u>. __aren't ready__

12. If I get the job, I'll be <u>walking on air</u>. __proud__

13. My friend's business is <u>on the skids</u>. __is good__

14. George's ideas are <u>off the wall</u>. __bad__

15. That's enough silliness. Let's <u>talk turkey</u>. __talk seriously__

16. Victor was <u>in hot water</u> for not cleaning the garage. __in trouble__

17. The audience was <u>all ears</u> when you spoke. __paying attentio__

18. The lost book <u>turned up</u> yesterday. __showed up__

19. Jan and I <u>put our heads together</u> to solve the problem. __worked together__

Unit 1: Vocabulary
Core Skills Grammar Review

Figurative Language

> **Figurative language** describes one thing in terms of another and is not meant to be taken literally. Types of figurative language include personification, allusions, verbal irony, puns, euphemisms, oxymoron, hyperbole, and paradox.
>
> **Personification** gives human characteristics to nonhuman things.
>
> **Example:** A falling leaf **danced cheerfully** on the breeze.
>
> An **allusion** is a reference to a person, place, or event from history, literature, religion, mythology, sports, science, or popular culture.
>
> **Example:** At this time when so many are in need, let us not forget the **lessons of one Ebenezer Scrooge.**

Underline each example of personification.

1. The train eats up the miles as it chugs along the countryside.

2. The sun was smiling down on our cookout.

3. After the earthquake, a lone skyscraper stood stubbornly in the city skyline.

4. Jeanette coaxed and coaxed, but the pizza dough refused to rise.

5. We watched as the afternoon sky spread its angry clouds over the city.

Underline each allusion.

6. They fell in love as fast as Romeo and Juliet, but fell out of love just as fast.

7. Jason was a good soccer player, but his lack of discipline turned out to be his Achilles heel.

8. Living near those mountains is like having a Garden of Eden in my own backyard.

9. When Bethany gets overwhelmed, she always exclaims, "Beam me up, Scotty!"

10. Mr. McCoy is very aggressive in the way he runs his business; I think he has a Napoleon complex.

Write personification or allusion to identify the type of figurative language.

11. The flower turned its gaze toward the sun. _____

12. Filing a lawsuit against that company would be like fighting Goliath. _____

13. With open arms, the cozy chair beckoned me. _____

14. Earth can support life because it is in the Goldilocks zone. _____

15. The ocean waves sang soft songs in their gentle, rhythmic tones. _____

Verbal irony occurs when there is a contrast between what is said and what is actually meant.

    Example: Nick played a great game; he only struck out five times.

A **pun** is a play on words meant to be humorous. Some puns are based on multiple meanings of one word, while others play on two words that sound alike but have different meanings.

    Example: Swiss cheese must be good for you because it is **holesome**.

A **euphemism** is an agreeable-sounding term that is substituted for another word or phrase that might seem too direct or blunt. Some euphemisms are used to avoid hurting people's feelings. Others might be used to mislead people or to hide unpleasant truths.

    Example: The little girl's hamster has **passed away.** (died)

An **oxymoron** combines two contradictory words into one term or phrase, usually to create a special effect.

    Example: Grounding me for skateboarding without my helmet was Dad's idea of **tough love**.

Write the kind of figurative language used in each sentence: <u>verbal irony</u>, <u>pun</u>, <u>euphemism</u>, or <u>oxymoron</u>.

16. Oh, I absolutely *love* that hat! Are those real grapes? _____

17. The city's sanitation engineers empty thousands of trash bins every day. _____

18. Oh, that dog must have such a hard life. Look at all those treats and toys! _____

19. The lot is full of certified pre-owned vehicles that are for sale. _____

20. Trying to write with a broken pencil is pointless. _____

21. Could you show me to the powder room, please? _____

22. I could not stand another moment of the deafening silence. _____

23. Unfortunately their family is a bit income-challenged. _____

24. Police were called to a daycare because a three-year-old was resisting a rest. _____

25. Karli was so tired she felt like the walking dead. _____

26. The company may let a number of employees go to save costs. _____

27. She's such a great friend that she stole my idea and took credit for it. _____

28. What a charming man. He almost ran me over and then glared at me. _____

29. I was trying to understand how lightning works, and suddenly it struck me. _____

30. It was such an emotional wedding that even the cake was in tiers. _____

31. The misunderstood child often felt alone in a crowd. _____

32. Oh, don't hurry; I *enjoy* waiting for you all afternoon. _____

33. A noun and a verb started dating, but it didn't work out. The noun was too possessive. _____

A **hyperbole** uses obvious exaggeration to emphasize a point, express strong emotion, or create a comic effect. Hyperboles are not meant to be taken literally.

Example: They pulled up in a limousine the length of a city block.

A **paradox** is a statement or situation that seems to be a contradiction but reveals a truth.

Example: It is always darkest before the dawn.

Write hyperbole or paradox to identify the type of figurative language.

34. The more things change, the more they stay the same. _____

35. His father looks tall enough to touch the clouds. _____

36. The heat was so intense my skin was melting off. _____

37. We watched a parade a thousand miles long. _____

38. Whatever doesn't kill you will make you stronger. _____

39. My brain nearly exploded from the effort of taking that test. _____

40. Molly has enough friends to fill a football stadium. _____

41. The best teachers allow themselves to become students of their students. _____

42. It's so cold there are polar bears walking around in down jackets. _____

43. At that moment, the homeless man thought himself to be the richest man alive. _____

Write your own hyperbole to complete each sentence.

44. That jacket is older than _____.

45. I am so tired I could sleep for _____.

46. The food was good, but the servings were the size of _____.

47. I've heard that story _____ times!

48. These shoes are so tight that _____.

49. The sandwich buns at that restaurant are the size of _____.

50. She was so embarrassed her face turned as red as _____.

51. Wow! That snake must have been _____ long!

52. The geese we saw at the lake were as big as _____.

53. In fact, I'm so hungry I could eat _____.

Word Relationships

An **analogy** is a comparison of two pairs of words that have the same relationship.

Example: The analogy **skeleton : body :: frame : building** is read "skeleton is to body as frame is to building," and it shows the relationship of a part to a whole. The skeleton is a part of the body in much the same way as the frame is part of a building.

Understanding the relationship between words can help you better understand each of the words. Analogies can show different types of word relationships.

Relationship	Analogy
part to whole	card : deck :: letter : word
cause and effect	humor : laughter :: pain : tears
synonyms	shy : timid :: happy : joyous
antonyms	smooth : rough :: peaceful : turbulent
item to category	apple : fruit :: giraffe : mammal

Tell what relationship the word pairs show. Use the chart above.

1. germs : infection :: cleanliness: health _____

2. cotton : fiber :: wheat : grain _____

3. foolish : silly :: rapid : fast _____

4. carelessness : accident :: awareness : safety _____

5. love : hate :: consensus : disagreement _____

6. sandal : shoe :: novel : literature _____

7. lightbulb : lamp :: keyboard : laptop _____

8. rural : urban :: flexible : rigid _____

Write the word from the box that completes each analogy.

savings	courageous	accept	waste
molecule	knowledge	color	government

9. lead : follow :: reject : _____

10. loss : sorrow :: frivolousness : _____

11. feather : wing :: atom : _____

12. ashamed : proud :: cowardly : _____

13. reunion : joy :: conservation : _____

14. leaf : tree :: legislator : _____

15. exploration : discovery :: research : _____

16. Monarch : butterfly :: magenta : _____

Unit 1 Review

Using the homonyms in parentheses, write the correct words on the lines.

1. (week, weak) Anna was _____ for a _____ after she had the flu.

2. (blew, blue) The wind _____ leaves and twigs into the beautiful _____ water.

3. (read, red) Meg _____ a poem about a young girl with _____ hair and freckles.

4. (pane, pain) Ed felt a _____ in his hand when he removed the broken window _____.

Circle the letter of the best definition for each underlined homograph.

5. John <u>flies</u> to California every summer to visit his family.

    a. insects   **b.** moves in the air

6. Mr. Bailey owns a fruit and vegetable <u>stand</u>.

    a. to be on one's feet   **b.** a small open structure

7. Don't forget to <u>wind</u> the alarm clock before you go to bed.

    a. to tighten a spring   **b.** air movement

Choose an appropriate prefix or suffix from the box for each of the underlined words below. Write the new word on the line.

dis-	mis-	re-	un-	-ish	-ful	-less	-en

8. full of <u>thanks</u> _____

9. to <u>pay</u> again _____

10. to not <u>agree</u> _____

11. acting like a <u>fool</u> _____

12. to make <u>black</u> in color _____

13. without <u>thanks</u> _____

14. not <u>happy</u> _____

15. <u>take</u> wrongly _____

Write <u>S</u> before each pair of synonyms. Write <u>A</u> before each pair of antonyms.

_____ 16. quiet, noisy   _____ 19. calm, peaceful   _____ 22. cry, weep

_____ 17. fearless, brave   _____ 20. lost, found   _____ 23. bottom, top

_____ 18. begin, start   _____ 21. night, day   _____ 24. dull, sharp

Write a short definition of the underlined word based on the context clues. Use a dictionary if necessary.

25. He finally overcame his overriding <u>phobia</u>, or fear, of heights.

_____

26. <u>Fabrications</u> can run the range from "little white lies" to outrageous "whoppers."

_____

27. I didn't want to get into an argument, but Ted insisted on being <u>contentious</u>.

_____

Write (−) if the underlined word has a negative connotation. Write (+) if the underlined word has a positive connotation.

_____ **28.** Joe is sometimes <u>narrow-minded</u>.

_____ **29.** Marie is very <u>outgoing</u>.

_____ **30.** Do you like to <u>gossip</u>?

_____ **31.** Let's <u>donate</u> this later.

_____ **32.** I <u>demand</u> that you listen to me.

_____ **33.** The <u>palace</u> was very grand.

Underline the more precise or vivid word choice in parentheses.

34. My dog has a (good, charming) personality.

35. The (comforting, nice) tone of my sister's voice always calms me down.

36. The cat (leapt, jumped) from the chair and (ran, scurried) across the floor.

37. Then John drove up in a (cool, vintage) (car, convertible).

Underline the idiom in each sentence. Then write what the idiom means.

38. Since there was little time, the mayor only hit the high spots of his speech.

_____

39. The committee's bank account was low, so they had to cut corners on their party.

_____

40. Mark couldn't find a job, so he asked his uncle to pull some strings for him.

_____

Write the kind of figurative language used in each sentence. Choose from the types shown in the box.

personification	allusion	verbal irony	euphemism	hyperbole

41. Her face was as white as the snow on the ground. _____

42. This weekend was such a blast; I spent most of it studying. _____

43. The wild grasses whispered mysteriously in the wind. _____

44. Today our beloved dog Buddy passed on from this world. _____

Write the word from the box that completes each analogy.

athlete	frigid	gratitude	reveal	fabric

45. fall : climb :: hide : _____

46. injury : pain :: gift : _____

47. bird : flock :: thread : _____

48. soft : spongy :: cold : _____

Using What You've Learned

Write a sentence using a homonym for each word.

1. new _____

2. grater _____

3. choose _____

4. waist _____

For each homograph below, write two sentences. Be sure to use a different meaning of the homograph in each sentence.

5. light   **a.** _____

          b. _____

6. shed   **a.** _____

          b. _____

Add one of the following prefixes or suffixes to each base word to make a new word.

> **Prefixes:** in-, non-, dis-, mis-, pre-, re-   **Suffixes:** -able, -ful, -less

7. place _____   12. tire _____

8. direct _____   13. remark _____

9. use _____   14. spell _____

10. measure _____   15. pay _____

11. speech _____   16. fund _____

Rewrite the following sentences using synonyms for the underlined words.

17. <u>Blasts</u> of wind whistled through the <u>openings</u> between the boards on the window.

_____

18. Then a <u>hush</u> seemed to fall over our part of the <u>world</u>.

_____

Rewrite the following sentences using antonyms for the underlined words.

19. <u>Black</u> clouds drifted across the <u>evening</u> sky.

_____

20. The <u>heavy</u> wind was blowing leaves <u>over</u> the trees.

_____

Write a short definition of the underlined word based on the context clues. Use a dictionary if necessary.

21. I'm not sure if my plan is <u>feasible</u>, but I'd like to try it.

_____

22. Some of the paintings were serious, but most of them seemed rather <u>frivolous</u>.

_____

23. The frightened child answered in a small, <u>tremulous</u> voice.

_____

Think of words that have almost the same meaning as the neutral word, but have a more negative or positive connotation. Complete the chart with your words.

Negative Connotation	Neutral	Positive Connotation
24. _____	thin	**27.** _____
25. _____	old	**28.** _____
26. _____	clothes	**29.** _____

Rewrite each sentence, adding details and using vivid, precise language.

30. Kara's truck looks good and runs well.

_____

31. The room was filled with stuff.

_____

32. The forest animals tried to escape the fire.

_____

Use the following idioms in sentences. Use a dictionary if necessary.

33. throw in the towel _____

_____

34. skating on thin ice _____

_____

35. get in touch with _____

_____

Rewrite each sentence using the type of figurative language shown in parentheses.

36. The sun was bright. (personification) _____

_____

37. That dog is dumb. (euphemism) _____

_____

38. I did not like sitting through that boring movie. (verbal irony) _____

_____

Recognizing Sentences

A **sentence** is a group of words that expresses a complete thought.

Example: Marie sings well.

Some of the following groups of words are sentences, and some are not. Write <u>S</u> before each group that is a sentence. Punctuate each sentence with a period.

_____ 1. When the downhill skiing season begins ____

_____ 2. Last summer I visited my friend in New Jersey ____

_____ 3. From the very beginning of the first-aid lessons ____

_____ 4. One of the children from the neighborhood ____

_____ 5. A visiting musician played the organ ____

_____ 6. On the way to school this morning ____

_____ 7. "I love you, Mother," said Mike ____

_____ 8. The blue house at the corner of Maple Street ____

_____ 9. After Emily left, the phone rang off the hook ____

_____ 10. Speak distinctly and loudly so that you can be heard ____

_____ 11. I have finally learned to drive our car ____

_____ 12. This is William's tenth birthday ____

_____ 13. At the very last moment, we were ready ____

_____ 14. When you speak in front of people ____

_____ 15. The basket of fruit on the table ____

_____ 16. Please answer the telephone, Julia ____

_____ 17. Hurrying to class because he is late ____

_____ 18. The first thing in the morning ____

_____ 19. That mistake was costly and unfortunate ____

_____ 20. We are planning to build a new doghouse ____

_____ 21. The dog chased the cat up the tree ____

_____ 22. Daniel Boone was born in Pennsylvania ____

_____ 23. The giant cottonwood in our backyard ____

_____ 24. Marla, bring my notebook ____

_____ 25. On a stool beside the back door ____

_____ 26. Sometimes the noise from the street ____

_____ 27. Somewhere out of state ____

_____ 28. The band played a lively march ____

_____ 29. That flight arrived on time ____

_____ 30. Was cracked in dozens of places ____

Types of Sentences

A **declarative sentence** makes a statement. It is followed by a period(.).

    Example: Alicia is my cousin.

An **interrogative sentence** asks a question. It is followed by a question mark (?).

    Example: Where are you going?

An **imperative sentence** expresses a command or request. It is followed by a period (.).

    Example: Close the door.

An **exclamatory sentence** expresses strong emotion. It can also express a command or request that is made with great excitement. It is followed by an exclamation mark (!).

    Examples: How you frightened me! Look at that accident!

Write **D** for declarative, **IN** for interrogative, **IM** for imperative, or **E** for exclamatory before each sentence. Put the correct punctuation at the end of each sentence.

_____ 1. Everyone will be here by nine o'clock ____

_____ 2. Train your mind to do its work efficiently ____

_____ 3. How does a canal lock work ____

_____ 4. Prepare each day's assignment on time ____

_____ 5. Are we going to the game now ____

_____ 6. Who brought these delicious peaches ____

_____ 7. Our guests have arrived ____

_____ 8. What is meant by rotation of crops ____

_____ 9. Please bring a glass of water ____

_____ 10. Stop that noise ____

_____ 11. Always stand up straight ____

_____ 12. Who arranged these flowers ____

_____ 13. Anna, what do you have in that box ____

_____ 14. The Vikings were famous sailors ____

_____ 15. Have you solved all the problems in our lesson ____

_____ 16. Jack, hand me that wrench ____

_____ 17. What is the capital of California ____

_____ 18. Cultivate a pleasant manner ____

_____ 19. How is a pizza made ____

_____ 20. Block that kick ____

_____ 21. A nation is measured by the character of its people ____

_____ 22. Are you an early riser ____

_____ 23. Practice good table manners ____

© Houghton Mifflin Harcourt Publishing Company

Unit 2: Sentences
Core Skills Grammar Review

Simple Subjects and Predicates

> The **simple subject** of a sentence is the main word in the complete subject. The simple subject is a noun or a word that stands for a noun.
>
> **Example:** My **sister** /lost her gloves.
>
> Sometimes the simple subject is also the complete subject.
>
> **Example:** **She**/lost her gloves.
>
> The **simple predicate** of a sentence is a verb within the complete predicate. The simple predicate may be a one-word verb or a verb of more than one word.
>
> **Examples:** She/**lost** her gloves. She/**is looking** for them.

Draw a slash between the complete subject and complete predicate in each sentence below. Underline the simple subject once and the simple predicate twice. The first one has been done for you.

1. A sudden clap of thunder / frightened all of us.
2. The soft snow covered the fields and roads.
3. We drove very slowly over the narrow bridge.
4. The students are making an aquarium.
5. Our class read about the founder of Hull House.
6. The women were talking in the park.
7. This album has many folk songs.
8. We are furnishing the sandwiches for tonight's picnic.
9. All the trees on that lawn are giant oaks.
10. Many Americans are working in foreign countries.
11. The manager read the names of the contest winners.
12. Bill brought these large melons.
13. We opened the front door of the house.
14. The two mechanics worked on the car for an hour.
15. Black and yellow butterflies fluttered among the flowers.
16. The child spoke politely.
17. We found many beautiful shells along the shore.
18. The best part of the program is the dance number.
19. Every ambitious person is working hard.
20. Sheryl swam across the lake two times.
21. Our program will begin promptly at eight o'clock.
22. The handle of this basket is broken.
23. The clock in the tower strikes every hour.
24. The white farmhouse on that road belongs to my cousin.
25. The first game of the season will be played tomorrow.

Complete Subjects and Predicates

Every sentence has two main parts, a **complete subject** and a **complete predicate**. The complete subject includes all the words that tell who or what the sentence is about.

    Examples: My brother/likes to go with us. **Six geese**/honked loudly.

Sometimes the simple subject is also the complete subject.

    Example: He/likes to go with us.

The complete predicate includes all the words that state the action or condition of the subject.

    Examples: My brother/**likes to go with us**. Six geese/**honked loudly**.

Sometimes the simple predicate is also the complete predicate.

    Example: Six geese/**honked**.

Draw a slash between the complete subject and the complete predicate in each sentence.

1. Bees fly.
2. Trains whistle.
3. A talented artist drew this cartoon.
4. The wind blew furiously.
5. My grandmother made this dress last year.
6. We surely have enjoyed the holiday.
7. This letter came to the post office box.
8. They rent a cabin in Colorado every summer.
9. Jennifer is reading about the pioneer days in the West.
10. Our baseball team won the third game of the series.
11. The band played a cheerful tune.
12. A cloudless sky is a great help to a pilot.
13. The voice of the auctioneer was heard throughout the hall.
14. A sudden flash of lightning startled us.
15. The wind howled down the chimney.
16. Their apartment is on the sixth floor.
17. We have studied many interesting places.
18. Each player on the team deserves credit for the victory.
19. Forest rangers fought the raging fire.
20. A friend taught Robert a valuable lesson.
21. Millions of stars make up the Milky Way.
22. Many of the children waded in the pool.
23. Yellowstone Park is a large national park.
24. Cold weather is predicted for tomorrow.

Write a sentence by adding a complete predicate to each complete subject.

25. All of the students _____

26. Elephants _____

27. The top of the mountain _____

28. The television programs tonight _____

29. I _____

30. Each of the girls _____

31. My father's truck _____

32. The dam across the river _____

33. Our new car _____

34. You _____

35. The books in our bookcase _____

36. The mountains _____

37. Today's blog post _____

38. The magazine staff _____

Write a sentence by adding a complete subject to each complete predicate.

39. _____ is a city in Mexico.

40. _____ came to our play.

41. _____ is a valuable mineral.

42. _____ grow beside the road.

43. _____ traveled day and night.

44. _____ was a great inventor.

45. _____ wrote the letter of complaint.

46. _____ met us at the airport.

47. _____ made potato salad for the picnic.

48. _____ made a nest in our tree.

49. _____ lives near the shopping center.

50. _____ have a meeting on Saturday.

Unit 2: Sentences
Core Skills Grammar Review

Name _____   Date _____

Compound Subjects

A **compound subject** is made up of two or more simple subjects.

    Example: Henri and **Tanya** / are tall people.

Draw a slash between the complete subject and the complete predicate in each sentence. Write <u>SS</u> for a simple subject. Write <u>CS</u> for a compound subject. The first one has been done for you.

____CS____	1. Arturo and I / often work late on Friday.
_____	2. Sandy left the person near the crowded exit.
_____	3. She and I will mail the packages to San Francisco, California, today.
_____	4. Shanghai and New Delhi are two cities visited by the group.
_____	5. The fire spread rapidly to other buildings in the neighborhood.
_____	6. Luis and Lenora helped their parents with the chores.
_____	7. Swimming, jogging, and hiking were our favorite sports.
_____	8. Melbourne and Sydney are important Australian cities.
_____	9. Eric and I had an interesting experience Saturday.
_____	10. The Red Sea and the Mediterranean Sea are connected by the Suez Canal.
_____	11. The Republicans and the Democrats made many speeches before the election.
_____	12. The people waved to us from the top of the cliff.
_____	13. Liz and Jim crated the freshly picked apples.
_____	14. Clean clothes and a neat appearance are important in an interview.
_____	15. The kitten and the old dog are good friends.
_____	16. David and Paul are on their way to the swimming pool.
_____	17. Tom combed his dog's shiny black coat.
_____	18. Redbud and dogwood trees bloom in the spring.
_____	19. I hummed a cheerful tune on the way to the meeting.
_____	20. Buffalo, deer, and antelope once roamed the plains of North America.
_____	21. Gina and Hiroshi raked the leaves.
_____	22. Brasilia and São Paulo are two cities in Brazil.
_____	23. Hang gliding is a popular sport in Hawaii.
_____	24. Our class went on a field trip to the aquarium.
_____	25. The doctor asked him to get a blood test.

Write two sentences containing compound subjects.

26. _____

27. _____

Unit 2: Sentences
Core Skills Grammar Review

Compound Predicates

> A **compound predicate** is made up of two or more simple predicates.
>
> **Example:** Joseph / **dances and sings**.

Draw a slash between the complete subject and the complete predicate in each sentence. Write SP for each simple predicate. Write CP for each compound predicate. The first one has been done for you.

<u>__CP__</u>   **1.** Edward / grinned and nodded.

_____   **2.** Plants need air to live.

_____   **3.** Old silver tea kettles were among their possessions.

_____   **4.** My sister buys and sells real estate.

_____   **5.** Snow covered every highway in the area.

_____   **6.** Mr. Sanders designs and makes odd pieces of furniture.

_____   **7.** Popcorn is one of my favorite snack foods.

_____   **8.** Soccer is one of my favorite sports.

_____   **9.** The ducks quickly crossed the road and found the ducklings.

_____   **10.** They came early and stayed late.

_____   **11.** Crystal participated in the Special Olympics this year.

_____   **12.** José raked and sacked the leaves.

_____   **13.** Perry built the fire and cooked supper.

_____   **14.** We collected old newspapers for the recycling center.

_____   **15.** Doug arrived in Toronto, Ontario, during the afternoon.

_____   **16.** Tony's parents are visiting Oregon and Washington.

_____   **17.** The Garzas live in that apartment building on Oak Street.

_____   **18.** The shingles were picked up and delivered today.

_____   **19.** The audience talked and laughed before the performance.

_____   **20.** Automobiles crowd and jam that highway early in the morning.

_____   **21.** The apples are rotting in the boxes.

_____   **22.** The leader of the group grumbled and scolded.

_____   **23.** She worked hard and waited patiently.

_____   **24.** Martin Luther King, Jr., was a great civil rights activist.

_____   **25.** The supervisor has completed the work for the week.

Write two sentences containing compound predicates.

26. _____

27. _____

Combining Sentences

Two sentences in which the subjects are different and the predicates are the same can be combined into one sentence. The two subjects are joined by <u>and</u>.

    Example: Hurricanes are storms. **Tornadoes** are storms. **Hurricanes and tornadoes** are storms.

Two sentences in which the subjects are the same and the predicates are different can be combined into one sentence. The two predicates may be joined by <u>or</u>, <u>and</u>, or <u>but</u>.

    Example: Hurricanes **begin over tropical oceans**. Hurricanes **move inland**. Hurricanes **begin over tropical oceans and then move inland**.

Combine each pair of sentences below. Underline the compound subject or the compound predicate in each sentence that you write.

1. Lightning is part of a thunderstorm. Thunder is part of a thunderstorm.

_____

2. Thunderstorms usually happen in the spring. Thunderstorms bring heavy rains.

_____

3. Depending on how close or far away it is, thunder sounds like a sharp crack. Depending on how close or far away it is, thunder rumbles.

_____

4. Lightning is very exciting to watch. Lightning can be very dangerous.

_____

5. Lightning causes many fires. Lightning harms many people.

_____

6. Open fields are unsafe places to be during a thunderstorm. Golf courses are unsafe places to be during a thunderstorm.

_____

7. Benjamin Franklin wanted to protect people from lightning. Benjamin Franklin invented the lightning rod.

_____

8. A lightning rod is placed on the top of a building. A lightning rod is connected to the ground by a cable.

_____

Independent and Dependent Clauses

A **clause** is a group of words that contains a subject and a predicate. There are two kinds of clauses: **independent clauses** and **dependent clauses**.

An **independent clause** can stand alone as a sentence because it expresses a complete thought.
    Example: The students came in when the bell rang. **The students came in.**

Underline the independent clause in each sentence below.

1. Frank will be busy because he is studying.
2. I have only one hour that I can spare.
3. The project must be finished when I get back.
4. Gloria volunteered to do the typing that needs to be done.
5. The work is going too slowly for us to finish on time.
6. Before Nathan started to help, I didn't think we could finish.
7. What else should we do before we relax?
8. Since you forgot to give this page to Gloria, you can type it.
9. After she had finished typing, we completed the project.
10. We actually got it finished before the deadline arrived.

A **dependent clause** has a subject and predicate but cannot stand alone as a sentence because it does not express a complete thought. A dependent clause must be combined with an independent clause to make a sentence.
    Example: The stamp **that I bought** was already in my collection.

Underline the dependent clause in each sentence below.

11. The people who went shopping found a great sale.
12. Tony's bike, which is a mountain bike, came from that store.
13. Juana was sad when the sale was over.
14. Marianne was excited because she wanted some new things.
15. Thomas didn't find anything since he went late.
16. The mall where we went shopping was new.
17. The people who own the stores are proud of the beautiful setting.
18. The mall, which is miles away, is serviced by the city bus.
19. We ran down the street because the bus was coming.
20. We were panting because we had run fast.

Adjective and Adverb Clauses

An **adjective clause** is a dependent clause that modifies a noun or a pronoun. It answers the question
Which one? or What kind? It usually modifies the word directly preceding it. Most adjective clauses
begin with a **relative pronoun**. A relative pronoun relates an adjective clause to the noun or pronoun
that the clause modifies. Who, whom, whose, which, and that are relative pronouns. An adjective
clause that starts with a relative pronoun is sometimes called a **relative clause.**

> **Example:** Always do the work **that is assigned to you.**
> ⌊_____⌋
> adjective clause

An **adverb clause** is a dependent clause that modifies a verb, an adjective, or another adverb. It
answers the question How? Under what condition? or Why? Words that introduce adverb clauses are
called **subordinating conjunctions**. The many subordinating conjunctions include such words as
when, after, before, since, although, and because.

> **Example:** We left **when the storm clouds gathered.**
> ⌊_____⌋
> adverb clause

**Underline the dependent clause. Then write underline adjective or underline adverb on the line.
Circle each relative pronoun.**

_____ **1.** John Paul Jones was a hero whose bravery won many victories.

_____ **2.** The person who reads the most books will get a prize.

_____ **3.** He overslept because he hadn't set the alarm.

_____ **4.** Give a rousing cheer when our team comes off the field.

_____ **5.** The picnic that we planned was canceled.

Add a dependent clause beginning with the word in parentheses to each independent clause below.

6. The package was gone (when) _____

_____

7. A depot is a place (where) _____

_____

8. Brad and I cannot go now (because) _____

_____

9. Tell me the name of the person (who) _____

_____

Compound and Complex Sentences

A **compound sentence** consists of two or more independent clauses. Each independent clause in a compound sentence can stand alone as a separate sentence. The independent clauses are usually joined by <u>and</u>, <u>but</u>, <u>so</u>, <u>or</u>, <u>for</u>, or <u>yet</u> and a comma.

Example: I like to dance, but Jim likes to sing.

Sometimes a **semicolon (;)** is used to join the independent clauses in a compound sentence.

Example: I like to dance; Jim likes to sing.

A **complex sentence** consists of one independent clause and one or more dependent clauses.

Example: <u>**When the fire alarm went off**</u>, everyone left the building.

dependent clause

Write <u>CP</u> before each compound sentence. Write <u>CX</u> before each complex sentence.

___CP___ 1. Our team didn't always win, but we always tried to be good sports.

___CP___ 2. You may stay, but I am going home.

___CX___ 3. The rangers who serve in Yellowstone Park know every inch of the ground.

___CP___ 4. That statement may be correct, but it isn't very polite.

___CX___ 5. We will meet whenever we can.

___CP___ 6. The pass was thrown perfectly, but Carlos was too well guarded to catch it.

___CX___ 7. The toga was worn by ancient Roman youths when they reached the age of twelve.

___CX___ 8. That song, which is often heard on the radio, was written years ago.

___CP___ 9. They cannot come for dinner, but they will be here later.

___CP___ 10. My brother likes dogs, but I prefer cats.

___CP___ 11. The engine is the heart of the submarine, and the periscope is the eye.

___CX___ 12. I will call you when it arrives.

___CX___ 13. Those people who camped here were messy.

___CX___ 14. Edison was only thirty years old when he invented the talking machine.

___CP___ 15. She crept silently, for she was afraid.

___CP___ 16. Move the table, but be careful with it.

___CX___ 17. Bolivia is the only South American country that does not have a port.

___CX___ 18. How many stars were in the flag that Key saw "by the dawn's early light"?

___CX___ 19. The octopus gets its name from two Greek words that mean <u>eight</u> and <u>feet</u>.

___CP___ 20. You may place the order, but we cannot guarantee shipment.

___CX___ 21. After the sun set, we built a campfire.

___CP___ 22. We made hamburgers for dinner, and then we toasted marshmallows.

___CP___ 23. Some people sang songs; others played games.

___CX___ 24. When it started to rain, everyone took shelter in their tents.

Unit 2: Sentences
Core Skills Grammar Review

Put brackets [ ] around each independent clause in the sentences below. Then underline the simple subject once and the simple predicate twice in each clause. The first one has been done for you.

25. [The <u>streets</u> <u><u>are</u></u> filled with cars], but [the <u>sidewalks</u> <u><u>are</u></u> empty].

26. [Those apples <u>are</u> too sour to eat], but [those pears are perfect.]

27. [<u>She</u> studies hard], but [<u>she</u> saves some time to enjoy herself.]

28. [<u>They</u> lost track of time], so [<u>they</u> <u>were</u> late.]

29. [<u>Eric</u> had not studied], so [<u>he</u> failed the test.]

30. [Yesterday it <u>rained</u> all day], but [today the <u>sun</u> is <u>shining</u>.]

31. [I set the alarm to get up early], but [<u>I</u> couldn't get up.]

32. [They may <u>sing</u> and dance until dawn], but [<u>they</u> will be <u>exhausted</u>.]

33. [My friend moved to Texas], and [<u>I</u> will miss her.]

34. [They arrived at the theater early], but [<u>there</u> <u>was</u> still a long line.]

35. [Lisa took her dog to the veterinarian], but [his office <u>was</u> closed.]

36. [The <u>black cat</u> leaped], but [fortunately it didn't catch the bird.]

37. [I found a baseball in the bushes], and [<u>I</u> gave it to my brother.]

38. [We loaded the cart with groceries], and [<u>we</u> went to the checkout.]

39. [The <u>stadium</u> <u>was</u> showered with lights], but [the <u>stands</u> <u>were</u> empty.]

40. [The small child whimpered], and [her mother hugged her.]

41. [The dark <u>clouds</u> rolled in], and [then <u>it</u> began to rain.]

In each complex sentence below, underline each dependent clause.

42. The hummingbird is the only bird <u>that can fly backward</u>.

43. The cat <u>that is sitting in the window</u> is mine.

44. The car <u>that is parked outside</u> is new.

45. Jack, <u>who is a football star,</u> is class president.

46. Bonnie, <u>who is an artist,</u> is also studying computer science.

47. John likes food <u>that is cooked in the microwave</u>.

48. The composer <u>who wrote the music</u> comes from Germany.

49. We missed seeing him <u>because we were late</u>.

50. <u>When Jake arrives,</u> we will tell him <u>what happened.</u>

60. She walked slowly <u>because she had hurt her leg</u>.

61. <u>When she walked to the podium,</u> everyone applauded.

62. <u>If animals could talk,</u> they might have a lot to tell.

63. Many roads <u>that were built in our city</u> are no longer traveled.

64. My address book, <u>which is bright red,</u> is gone.

65. Ann, <u>who is from Georgia,</u> just started working here today.

66. The crowd cheered <u>when the player came to bat</u>.

67. <u>When he hit the ball,</u> everyone stood up and yelled wildly.

Compound-Complex Sentences

A **compound-complex** sentence consists of two or more independent clauses and at least one dependent clause.

Example: Matt would have broken the school record, but he stumbled as he neared the finish line.
  independent clause   independent clause   dependent clause

In each compound-complex sentence below, put brackets around each independent clause and underline each dependent clause. The first one has been done for you.

1. <u>When Antonina came to this country</u>, [she enjoyed her new freedom], but [she also worked very hard.]

2. Cece went to Chile during the winter break, but her brother stayed home because he had made plans with friends.

3. Vegetarians, who do not eat meat, should watch their diets; they should eat nutritionally balanced meals.

4. Although they were both tired, Rosa went to her soccer practice, and Carl went to his piano lesson.

5. When Mr. Tolstoi entered the United States, he knew only a few words of English, but his wife was fluent in the language.

6. The two teens had avoided injury because they had worn their seat belts, but the driver of the other car was not as fortunate.

7. You should shut the gate whenever you leave the backyard; otherwise, the dogs may get out.

8. As we left the library, the rain pelted down, so we rushed back inside.

9. When we went to the science museum, we attended a lecture on electricity; after the lecture, we visited some of the exhibits.

10. The two dogs barked constantly until the sun rose; consequently, none of us got much sleep last night.

Write <u>CC</u> before each compound-complex sentence. Write <u>No</u> if the sentence is not a compound-complex sentence.

_____ 11. If you are a surfer, you may enjoy skateboarding too, because the sports are similar.

_____ 12. I was trying to entertain Jamal when I told him that joke, but he did not find it funny.

_____ 13. I was glad that the bus came early; I needed extra time to set up my exhibit.

_____ 14. Some scenes in the movie became too scary for me, so I excused myself and went to the lobby.

Correcting Fragments

A **sentence fragment** is a word group that looks like a complete sentence but does not contain both a subject and a verb or does not express a complete thought.

    Examples: Was speaking to the neighbors. (no subject) The man with the small dog. (no verb) After the crowd has thinned. (not a complete thought)

Sentence fragments can be corrected by (1) adding a subject, (2) adding a verb, or (3) attaching the fragment to a complete sentence.

    Examples: Kevin was speaking to the neighbors. The man with the small dog **walks by here every day. We will go to the festival** after the crowd has thinned.

Write F for a sentence fragment. Write S for a complete sentence.

_____ 1. Antonio and his friends in the bay.

_____ 2. They spotted a shark.

_____ 3. One of the sailboats nearby.

_____ 4. The swimmers could only see the fin on the shark's back.

_____ 5. As soon as they were safe on the shore.

Correct each sentence fragment below.

6. The two energetic boys and their little sister.

_____

7. Flew rapidly from tree to tree.

_____

8. As we carved the ice sculpture.

_____

9. Scurried by and hid in the hollow of an old log.

_____

10. A film crew of about twenty people.

_____

11. Even though she had slept well.

_____

12. All the students in that class.

_____

13. Because the snow was getting deeper.

_____

14. Studied two hours for the math test.

_____

Correcting Run-on Sentences

Two or more independent clauses that are run together without the correct punctuation are called a **run-on sentence**.

Example: The music was deafening I turned down the volume.

One way to correct a run-on sentence is to separate it into two sentences.

Example: The music was deafening. I turned down the volume.

Another way to correct a run-on sentence is to make it into a compound sentence.

Example: The music was deafening, so I turned down the volume.

Another way to correct a run-on sentence is to use a semicolon.

Example: The music was deafening; I turned down the volume.

Correct each run-on sentence below by writing it as two sentences or as a compound sentence.

1. The city council held a meeting a meeting is held every month.

_____

2. The council members are elected by the voters there are two thousand voters in the city.

_____

3. There is one council member from each suburb, the president is elected by the council members.

_____

4. Those who run for office must give speeches, the speeches should be short.

_____

5. The council decides on many activities every activity is voted on.

_____

6. Money is needed for many of the special activities, the council also plans fund-raisers in the city.

_____

7. The annual city picnic is sponsored by the city council the picnic is in May.

_____

Varying Sentences

Basic English sentences begin with a subject followed by a verb. However, using that pattern for every sentence makes writing dull. To make your writing more interesting, vary sentence beginnings.

Start some sentences with a single-word modifier.

> **Examples: Excitedly,** Kayla opened her presents. (adverb)
>
> **Hungry,** we stopped at a sandwich stand. (adjective)

Start some sentences with a modifying phrase.

> **Examples: With tears of joy,** Haley received her award. (prepositional phrase)
>
> **Smiling happily,** Tanya told us the good news. (participial phrase)
>
> **To make good grades,** you must study. (infinitive phrase)

Start some sentences with a subordinate clause.

> **Examples: Because the coach was angry,** the team ran ten laps. (adverb clause)
>
> **When she saw the puppy,** she fell in love with it. (adverb clause)

The following sentences are good, but they would make a boring paragraph. Rewrite each sentence using the type of sentence beginning shown in parentheses.

1. Animals are in danger of extinction in many parts of the world. (phrase)

_____

2. The aye-aye is related to the monkey, and it is a small animal. (phrase)

_____

3. The aye-aye is endangered because the rainforest on its home island is being destroyed. (dependent clause)

_____

4. You must travel to the Pyrenees, Portugal, or the former Soviet Union to see the desman, a water-dwelling mammal. (phrase)

_____

5. People are threatening the desman's survival by damming mountain streams. (phrase)

_____

6. The giant otter of South America is protected, but poachers still threaten its survival. (dependent clause)

_____

7. Mountain lions are cautious and generally stay away from humans. (single-word modifier)

_____

Combine simple sentences to create a compound sentence.

Example: The cat knocked over a lamp. The dog chewed up my shoe.

The cat knocked over a lamp, **and** the dog chewed up my shoe.

When you create a compound sentence, you are showing that the two ideas are **coordinate**, or equally important. Use the **coordinating conjunction** that shows the correct relationship.

Examples: *and* = similarity   *but* = contrast   *or* = choice   *so* = cause and effect

Combine the simple sentences to create a compound sentence that shows the relationship in parentheses.

8. Some Pueblos built villages in the valleys. Others settled in desert and mountain regions. (contrast)

_____

_____

9. Women gathered berries and other foods. Men hunted game. (similarity)

_____

_____

You can also combine simple sentences to create a complex sentence.

Examples: Some bats are dangerous. They rarely attack humans.

Although some people think bats are dangerous, they rarely attack humans.

When you create a complex sentence, you are showing that one idea is subordinate to, or less important than, the other. Use the subordinating word that shows the correct relationship.

Examples: *after* = time   *because* = cause and effect   *if* = condition

Combine the simple sentences to create a complex sentence. Use the subordinating word given in parentheses.

10. The Chickasaw caught fish using an interesting method. It involved poison. (that)

_____

_____

11. They threw the mild poison into a lake. The poison was made of walnut bark. (which)

_____

_____

45

Consistent Style and Tone

English can range from very formal to informal. A **formal style** is appropriate for serious papers and reports, tests, and business purposes. It uses exact words, technical language, and Standard English to create a serious and dignified tone. An **informal style** is appropriate for things like personal letters, journal entries, and less serious articles and essays. It uses simple, ordinary words and can include contractions, colloquialisms, and slang.

Examples: I have considered adopting a pet for quite some time. (formal)

I've been thinking about getting a pet for a while. (informal)

Choose a style based on your audience and purpose, and then keep the style consistent throughout your writing. Do not shift from one style to another.

Revise the paragraph using a consistent formal style and tone.

1.   The Sahara is one crazy huge desert, you know. It's this barren expanse of land dotted with sunbaked oases. One of the early oases was Taghaza. That was also called "the salt city." You heard me right. Would you believe the houses and mosques of Taghaza were made of blocks of salt? These salt-block buildings were roofed with camel skins. Although Taghaza was an unattractive village, its mines provided traders in the Mali kingdom with salt, and everybody around there wanted to get their hands on salt because it was way valuable.

_____

_____

_____

_____

_____

Revise the paragraph using a consistent informal style and tone.

2.   Well, I finally did it. I have officially completed the volunteer training at the animal shelter. What I have stated here is absolutely true. I will be permitted to begin volunteering next weekend. I am really into the idea of helping the homeless pets. I do believe I will enjoy walking the canine residents best, but I totally don't mind cleaning the cages and helping in the office too. My supervisor most days will be Mr. Ramirez. He's a fine human being with an excellent approach to his work. Great with the teen volunteers especially. I am extremely excited about this opportunity to serve.

_____

_____

_____

_____

_____

Parallel Structure

Use the same grammatical form to express ideas that go together. For example, use a noun with a noun, a phrase with a phrase, and a clause with a clause. This kind of balance in writing is called **parallel structure.**

    Examples: Gerry enjoys **reading** and **swimming**. (gerund with gerund)

    The dog scrambled **out the door**, **under the gate**, and **down the street**. (prepositional phrases with prepositional phrases)

    I believe **that she meant well** but **that she forgot the appointment**. (clause with a clause)

Underline the form in parentheses that will make the sentence parallel.

1. Jordan said (that you should get there early, to get there early) and that you should eat lunch first.

2. The River Thames runs through London and (to empty into the North Sea, empties into the North Sea).

3. Amanda enjoys soccer, tennis, and (baseball, playing baseball).

4. The teacher insisted that we study hard, (good behavior in class, that we behave well in class), and that we work together effectively.

5. Juanita is as good at knitting sweaters as she is at (model airplanes, building model airplanes).

Revise each sentence to create parallel structure.

6. Fernando is great at playing shortstop and to run the bases.

   _____

7. We wanted to see a play, eat at a Chinese restaurant, and walking around the plaza.

   _____

8. Vanessa was admired not only for her intelligence but she also had good business sense.

   _____

9. London is famous for its history, its culture, and having a lively theater district.

   _____

10. Rita spends more time with her family than being around her friends.

   _____

11. Houston has a busy business district, heavy traffic, and spreads across miles of suburbia.

   _____

12. The weather here in the springtime is often windy, hot, and with dry air.

   _____

13. I plan to play basketball, finish my homework, and my chores.

   _____

47

Unit 2 Review

Label each sentence as follows: Write <u>D</u> for declarative, <u>IN</u> for interrogative, <u>IM</u> for imperative, or <u>E</u> for exclamatory. Write <u>X</u> if it is not a sentence. Punctuate each sentence correctly.

_____ 1. Did you forget our appointment ____

_____ 2. Be careful ____

_____ 3. Rolled up our sleeping bags ____

_____ 4. All members will meet in this room ____

_____ 5. Help, I'm frightened ____

In each sentence below, underline the words that are identified in parentheses.

6. (complete subject) The lights around the public square went out.

7. (simple subject) Stations are in all parts of our country.

8. (complete predicate) We drove slowly across the bridge.

9. (simple predicate) We saw an unusual flower.

10. (compound predicate) Taro swims and dives quite well.

11. (compound subject) The cake and bread are kept in the box.

Label each sentence as follows: Write <u>CD</u> for a compound sentence. Write <u>CX</u> for a complex sentence. Write <u>CD-CX</u> for a compound-complex sentence.

12. The food that is needed for the picnic will be bought the day before. _____

13. Mary will get lettuce, but we may have some. _____

14. Jack, who said he would help, is late, and we have been waiting. _____

15. We will go, and they will meet us as soon as they can. _____

Underline the independent clause and circle the dependent clause in each sentence.

16. The campers got wet when it started raining.

17. The candidates that I voted for in the election won easily.

18. Before the board voted on the issue, it held public hearings.

Underline the dependent clause in each sentence. Write <u>adjective clause</u> or <u>adverb clause</u> on the line after each sentence.

19. Meteorologists are people who are trained in weather forecasting. _____

20. Before I decided on a college, I did many hours of research. _____

21. The experiment that I designed failed completely. _____

Revise each sentence fragment to make it a complete sentence.

22. Although the exam was challenging.

_____

23. Traveled to San Francisco frequently.

_____

24. A huge flock of black crows.

_____

Combine each pair of sentences to form a complex sentence.

25. The recycling trucks have been rescheduled. They usually run on Wednesday.

_____

26. We had to go to the recycling center every week. The city started curbside recycling.

_____

27. Our family has always recycled. We all believe it is the responsible thing to do.

_____

Revise each sentence to create parallel structure.

28. The boys ate at a pizza parlor, watched the baseball game, and to walk home.

_____

29. I look up to Daniel because he is wise and also for his strong sense of ethics.

_____

30. Tracy enjoys babysitting her sister more than to clean the house.

_____

49

Using What You've Learned

Read the sentences in the box. Then answer the questions below.

> **A.** Did I give you the tickets for the show?
>
> **B.** This compact disc is fantastic!
>
> **C.** Be at my house by seven o'clock.
>
> **D.** You and I can ride downtown together.
>
> **E.** We can stop and eat before the show.

1. _____ Which sentence has a compound subject?

2. _____ Which sentence has a compound predicate?

3. _____ Which sentence is interrogative?

4. _____ Which sentences are declarative?

5. _____ Which sentence is exclamatory?

6. _____ Which sentence is imperative?

7. What is the complete subject of E? _____

8. What is the simple subject of E? _____

9. What is the complete predicate of D? _____

Underline each independent clause and circle each dependent clause.

10. We put up decorations, but the streamers sagged after we hung them.

11. Mark knows party planning because he has many parties.

12. Everyone who wants to go to the party must bring something.

13. If everyone brings something, the party will be great.

14. Unless I am wrong, the party is tomorrow.

15. As if everything had been done, Jake ran out of the room.

16. The girls who planned the party received roses, and they were thrilled.

Combine each pair of sentences to form a compound sentence.

17. The team sat in the dugout. The fans sat in the stands.

18. The rain finally stopped. The game continued.

19. It was the bottom of the ninth inning. There were two outs.

20. The batter swung at the pitch. The umpire called, "Strike three!"

Create complex sentences by adding a dependent clause or an independent clause to each group of words.

21. She looked sad _____

22. When she thought about what she said _____

23. This was the time _____

24. After she wrote her apology _____

25. When she wrote it _____

26. Before we left the house _____

Rewrite the paragraph below, correcting the run-on sentences.

   In space medicine research, new types of miniature equipment for checking how the body functions have been developed on the spacecraft, astronauts' breathing rates, heartbeats, and blood pressure are taken with miniature devices no larger than a pill. These devices detect the information and transmit it to scientists back on Earth they allow the scientists to monitor astronauts' body responses from a long distance and over long periods of time.

27.

_____

_____

_____

_____

_____

_____

_____

Revise each sentence using the type of sentence beginning shown in parentheses.

28. We finally crawled into our sleeping bags. (single-word modifier)

_____

29. Dad was embarrassed by his awkwardness and rarely dated as a teenager. (phrase)

_____

30. A player must find all the treasures to move to the next level in that game. (phrase)

_____

31. The skies were dark and the air was breezy, but we did not get any rain. (dependent clause)

_____

32. Ferrets are curious and will explore every corner, cupboard, and drawer in the house. (single-word modifier)

_____

Common, Proper, and Collective Nouns

A **noun** is a word or word group used to name a person, place, or thing.
A **common noun** names any one of a class of things.

   Examples: woman, tree, city

A **proper noun** names a particular person, place, or thing. It begins with a capital letter.

   Examples: Ms. Patel, Chicago, Empire State Building

A **collective noun** names a group of persons or things.

   Examples: crowd, congress, public, Cayman Islands

Underline each noun. Then write C or P above it to show if it is a common or a proper noun. If the noun is also collective, write Coll. The first one has been done for you.

1. Maria is my sister.
2. Honolulu is the chief city and capital of Hawaii.
3. Rainbow Natural Bridge is hidden away in the wild mountainous part of southern Utah.
4. On Saturday my family visited a nearby museum.
5. The Declaration of Independence is often called the birth certificate of the United States.
6. Abraham Lincoln, Edgar Allan Poe, and Frederic Chopin were born in the same year.
7. The orchestra sounded wonderful, but the concert was long.
8. We watched a flock of geese flying over the Colorado River.

Write a proper noun suggested by each common noun.

9. country ___America___
10. governor ___Bill Haslam___
11. state ___Tennessee___
12. athlete ___Messi___
13. school ___Oak View Elementry___
14. actor ___Tom Cruise___
15. day ___Tuesday___
16. car ___Lamborghini___
17. lake ___Lake Michigan___
18. holiday ___Christmas___

Write a sentence using each proper noun and the common noun for its class. The first one has been done for you.

19. Mexico   Mexico is another country in North America.
20. December ___Christmas is in the month of December___
21. Alaska ___Alaska was purchased by the United States as a state.___
22. Thanksgiving Day ___Thanksgiving Day is a Holiday during November___
23. Barack Obama ___Barack Obama was elected as president in 2008.___
24. Tuesday ___Tuesday is the next day after Monday.___

Singular and Plural Nouns

The following chart shows how to change <u>singular nouns</u> into <u>plural nouns</u>.

Noun	Plural Form	Examples
Most nouns	Add -<u>s</u>	ship, ships nose, noses
Nouns ending in a consonant and -<u>y</u>	Change the -<u>y</u> to -<u>i</u> and add -<u>es</u>	sky, skies navy, navies
Nouns ending in -<u>o</u>	Add -<u>s</u> or -<u>es</u>	hero, heroes piano, pianos
Most nouns ending in -<u>f</u> or -<u>fe</u>	Change the -<u>f</u> or -<u>fe</u> to -ves	half, halves
Most nouns ending in -<u>ch</u>, -<u>sh</u>, -<u>s</u>, or -<u>x</u>	Add -es	bench, benches bush, bushes tax, taxes
Many two-word or three-word compound nouns	Add -<u>s</u> to the principle word	son-in-law, sons-in-law
Nouns with the same form in the singular and plural	No change	sheep

Fill in the blank with the plural form of the word in parentheses.

1. (brush)   These are plastic ___brushes___.

2. (lunch)   That cafe on the corner serves well-balanced ___lunches___.

3. (country)   What ___countries___ belong to the United Nations?

4. (bench)   There are many iron ___benches___ in the park.

5. (earring)   These ___earrings___ came from Italy.

6. (calf)   How many ___calves___ are in that pen?

7. (piano)   There are three ___pianos___ in the warehouse.

8. (fox)   Did you see the ___foxes___ at the zoo?

9. (daisy)   We bought Susan a bunch of ___daisies___.

10. (potato)   Do you like baked ___potatoes___?

11. (dish)   Please help wash the ___dishes___.

12. (store)   There are three ___stores___ near my house.

Write the correct plural form for each singular noun.

13. booklet _booklets_
14. tomato _tomatoes_
15. truck _trucks_
16. chef _chefs_
17. branch _branches_
18. toddler _toddlers_
19. penny _pennies_
20. potato _potatoes_
21. piece _pieces_
22. door _doors_
23. island _islands_
24. country _countries_
25. house _houses_
26. garage _garage_
27. fish _fishes_

28. watch _watches_
29. elf _____
30. desk _____
31. pan _____
32. sheep _____
33. garden _____
34. pony _____
35. solo _____
36. tree _____
37. light _____
38. church _____
39. city _____
40. spoonful _____
41. vacation _____
42. home _____

Rewrite the sentences, changing each underlined singular noun to a plural noun.

43. Put the <u>apple</u> and <u>orange</u> in the <u>box</u>.

_____

44. Jan wrote five <u>letter</u> to her <u>friend</u>.

_____

45. Those <u>building</u> each have four <u>elevator</u>.

_____

46. Our <u>family</u> drove many <u>mile</u> to get to the <u>lake</u>.

_____

47. The <u>top</u> of those <u>car</u> were damaged in the <u>storm</u>.

_____

48. My <u>aunt</u> and <u>uncle</u> attended the family reunion.

_____

Name _____ Date _____

Possessive Nouns

> A **possessive noun** shows possession of the noun that follows.
> Form the possessive of most singular nouns by adding an apostrophe (') and -s.
>
> **Examples:** the boy's hat   Mr. Thomas's car
>
> Form the possessive of a plural noun ending in -s by adding only an apostrophe.
>
> **Examples:** the Smiths' home   girls' bikes   sisters' names
>
> Form the possessive of a plural noun that does not end in -s by adding an apostrophe and -s.
>
> **Examples:** children's classes   men's books

Write the possessive form of each noun.

1. girl _____
2. child _____
3. women _____
4. children _____
5. John _____

6. baby _____
7. boys _____
8. teacher _____
9. Dr. Ray _____
10. ladies _____

11. brother _____
12. soldier _____
13. men _____
14. aunt _____
15. Ms. Jones _____

Rewrite each phrase using a possessive noun. The first one has been done for you.

16. the cap belonging to Jim   _____Jim's cap_____
17. the wrench that belongs to Kathy   _____
18. the smile of the baby   _____
19. the car that my friend owns   _____
20. the new shoes that belong to Kim   _____
21. the collar of the dog   _____
22. the golf clubs that Frank owns   _____
23. the shoes that belong to the runners _____
24. the friends of our parents   _____
25. the opinion of the editor   _____
26. the lunches of the children   _____
27. the coat belonging to Kyle   _____
28. the assignment of the teacher   _____

Noun Phrases

> A **noun phrase** consists of a noun plus all its modifiers.
>
> **Examples: The petunias in the garden** are splendid.
>
> **Those tomatoes** were grown by **local farmers**.
>
> **The kitten that we adopted** is sick.

Put parentheses around each noun phrase and underline the noun that the other words in the phrase modify.

1. The guest speaker gave a presentation about the migration of Monarch butterflies.

2. We took a long bike ride yesterday.

3. The bees are buzzing around the flowering bushes in their backyard.

4. The movie that I watched last night was not funny.

5. Lily has practiced her gymnastics routine over and over again.

6. Even after the heavy rains had stopped, the floodwaters remained high for days.

7. Jessie loves any books that have fantasy creatures or monsters in them.

8. A rowboat on a calm lake makes a romantic image.

9. This salad is tasty, but I would like some bread to go with it, please.

10. An old photograph of her grandparents hung on the living room wall.

11. That hike was grueling, but the beautiful view at the top of the mountain made it worthwhile.

12. The car that Mr. Keller bought should be very reliable.

13. Wildflowers grow along this trail in the spring.

14. Any idea that is fresh and interesting is worth considering.

15. Many players on the team have improved their skills.

16. Our solar system is only a tiny part of a vast galaxy.

17. A look at the full moon through a telescope can be mesmerizing.

18. Take your heavy coat with you on cold nights like this one.

19. I think that terrier mix is the best dog to adopt.

20. The produce stand on Highway 45 is busy today.

21. Books about farming have always fascinated Malik.

22. The apartment building on the corner is in need of repairs.

23. For this assignment we will need a computer that is fast and powerful.

24. The players on the other team showed good sportsmanship throughout the whole game.

25. The bats that live under that bridge fly out every night and eat insects.

26. Cynthia is always looking for a good book to read.

27. I like movies with complex characters and inspiring messages.

28. The chairs around that dining room table are all falling apart.

Noun Clauses

A **noun clause** is a dependent clause that is used as a noun. Noun clauses usually begin with <u>that</u>, <u>what</u>, <u>when</u>, <u>where</u>, <u>whether</u>, <u>who</u>, <u>whoever</u>, <u>whom</u>, <u>whomever</u>, <u>whose</u>, <u>why</u>, or <u>how</u>. A noun clause may be used as a subject, a predicate nominative, a direct object, an indirect object, or the object of a preposition.

> **Examples: How the pyramids were built** fascinates me. (subject)
>
> Is this **what you wanted?** (predicate nominative)
>
> I know **who will win the award.** (direct object)
>
> Give **whoever arrives first** the best seat. (indirect object)
>
> Scientists disagree about **why dinosaurs became extinct.** (object of a preposition)

Underline the noun clause in each sentence.

1. That they were angry was obvious to the others.

2. Three dollars was what Daniel offered for the trinket.

3. Anthony and Peter remembered who he was.

4. The hostess gives whoever enters a menu.

5. Eager to please the speaker, we listened to whatever he said.

6. We couldn't find what was making the noise.

7. Whatever you decide will be fine with us.

8. No, these results are not what we had planned.

9. Do you know why the team has lost so many games?

10. Stuart is looking for whoever owns that red bicycle.

11. Checking our supplies, we discovered that we had forgotten the flour.

12. The story's worst flaw is that it doesn't have a carefully developed plot.

13. Whoever takes us to the beach is my friend for life.

14. The painter gave whatever spots had dried on the wall another coat of primer.

15. At lunch, my friends and I talked about what we should do as our service project.

16. That Coretta Scott King spoke for peace surprised no one at the conference.

17. Whoever wins the student council election will have a great deal of responsibility.

18. Can you please tell me when the museum opens?

19. What I like most about Harriet is her cheerful personality.

20. Sometimes I am amused by what I read in online advice blogs.

21. Through scientific research, psychologists have learned that everyone dreams during sleep.

22. The problem is that my budget does not allow for many new clothes.

23. Do you know what the referees say to the captains at the beginning of the game?

24. I don't know how you made that difficult decision.

25. Whether we drive or take the train will depend on the schedule.

Appositives

An **appositive** is a noun that identifies or explains the noun or pronoun it follows.

> **Example:** My dog, **Fido**, won a medal.

An **appositive phrase** consists of an appositive and its modifiers.

> **Example:** My book, **a novel about the Civil War**, is one of the best I've read.

Use **commas** to set off an appositive or an appositive phrase that is not essential to the meaning of the sentence.

> **Example:** John Gray, **my uncle**, owns that home.

Don't use commas if the appositive is essential to the meaning of the sentence.

> **Examples:** My brother Kevin arrived late. My other brother Charlie arrived early.

Underline the appositive or appositive phrase and circle the noun that it identifies.

1. Banff, the large Canadian national park, is my favorite place to visit.
2. The painter Vincent Van Gogh cut off part of his ear.
3. The White House, home of the president of the United States, is open to the public for tours.
4. Uncle Marco, my mother's brother, is an engineer.
5. Earth, the only inhabited planet in our solar system, is home to a diverse population of plants and animals.
6. The scorpion, a native of the southwestern part of North America, has a poisonous sting.
7. Emily's prize Persian cat Amelia won first prize at the cat show.
8. Judge Andropov, the presiding judge, sentenced the criminal to prison.
9. Paula's friend from Florida, Luisa, watched a space shuttle launch.

Complete each sentence with an appropriate appositive.

10. My friend ____Jack_____ bought a new bike.
11. The bike, ____Firebolt 2000_____, is fast and sleek.
12. Joe and his friend _____Adi_____ plan to ride their bikes together.
13. They will ride to Pease Park, ____the biggest Park_____, on Saturday.
14. They plan to meet Anne, ____the superstar_____, on the bike path.
15. After bicycling, they will see a movie, ____the IT_____.
16. Our friend ____Jesse_____ might come with us.
17. We will get a snack, ____popcorn_____, to eat during the movie.
18. My favorite actor, ____Tom Cruise kohn_____, might be in the movie.

Verbs

A **verb** is a word that expresses action, being, or state of being.

> **Examples:** Leo traveled to Europe. Maura is an accountant.

A verb has four principal parts: **present**, **present participle**, **past**, and **past participle**.

For regular verbs, form the present participle by adding -<u>ing</u> to the present. Use a form of the helping verb <u>be</u> with the present participle.

Form the past and past participle by adding -<u>ed</u> to the present. Use a form of the helping verb <u>have</u> with the past participle.

Present	Present Participle	Past	Past Participle
listen	(is) listening	listened	(have, had, has) listened
help	(is) helping	helped	(have, had, has) helped
change	(is) changing	changed	(have, had, has) changed

Irregular verbs form their past and past participle in other ways. A dictionary shows the principal parts of these verbs.

Write the present participle, past, and past participle for each verb. The first one has been done for you.

PRESENT	PRESENT PARTICIPLE	PAST	PAST PARTICIPLE
1. scatter	(is) scattering	scattered	(have, had, has) scattered
2. express			
3. paint			
4. call			
5. cook			
6. observe			
7. look			
8. walk			
9. ramble			
10. shout			
11. notice			
12. order			
13. gaze			
14. borrow			
15. start			
16. work			

Verb Tenses

The **tense** of a verb tells the time of the action or being. There are three simple tenses— present, past, and future.

Present tense tells about what is happening now.
  Examples: Conrad **is** busy. Conrad **studies** hard.

Past tense tells about something that happened before.
  Example: Conrad **was** sick yesterday.

Future tense tells about something that will happen. The helping verbs <u>will</u> and <u>shall</u> are used in future tense.
  Examples: Conrad **will take** the test tomorrow. I **shall keep** my word.

Complete each sentence by writing a verb in the tense shown in parentheses.

1. (future) Hilary _____ tomorrow.

2. (future) Joe _____ her up at the airport.

3. (past) We _____ the house yesterday.

4. (past) Carl _____ reservations for tomorrow night.

5. (present) Hilary _____ my friend.

6. (future) We _____ on a sightseeing tour.

7. (present) I _____ very excited about Hilary's visit.

8. (past) Margaret _____ Toby last week.

Write <u>present</u>, <u>past</u>, or <u>future</u> for the tense of each underlined verb.

9. Classes <u>will end</u> next month.   _____

10. We <u>studied</u> hard yesterday.   _____

11. Final exams <u>will start</u> soon.   _____

12. I <u>review</u> every evening.   _____

13. This method <u>worked</u> at midterm.   _____

14. I <u>got</u> As on my tests then.   _____

15. Marty <u>studies</u> with me.   _____

16. We <u>will study</u> every evening this week.   _____

17. I hardly <u>studied</u> last year.   _____

18. My grades <u>showed</u> it, too.   _____

The **perfect tenses** express action that happened before another time or event.

The **present perfect** tense tells about something that happened at an indefinite time in the past. The present perfect tense consists of has or have + the past participle.

   Examples: I **have eaten** already. He **has eaten**, too.

The **past perfect** tense tells about something that happened before something else in the past. The past perfect tense consists of had + the past participle.

   Example: I already **had eaten** when they arrived.

Write present perfect or past perfect for the tense of the underlined verbs.

19. _____ Mei had completed high school in June.

20. _____ She had gone to college in Memphis before coming here.

21. _____ Mei has decided that she likes her new college.

22. _____ She had worried that she wouldn't fit in.

23. _____ Mei has lived in her house for eight months.

24. _____ We have tried to make Mei feel welcome.

25. _____ She has told us a great deal about Memphis.

26. _____ We had known Memphis was an important city.

27. _____ However, Mei has described things we never knew!

28. _____ We have decided that we would like to visit Tennessee some day.

Complete each sentence with have, has, or had to form the verb tense indicated in parentheses.

29. (present perfect)   The pitcher _____ left the mound.

30. (present perfect)   The coach and catcher _____ talked to him.

31. (past perfect)   The coach _____ warned him to be careful.

32. (present perfect)   Jason _____ taken his place on the mound.

33. (past perfect)   Jason _____ pitched ten games by the end of last season.

34. (present perfect)   Jason _____ pitched very well.

35. (past perfect)   The team _____ won every game until last week.

Verb Phrases

Some sentences contain a **verb phrase**. A verb phrase consists of a **main verb** and one or more other verbs.

Examples: The women **are singing**. Where **have** you **been?**

Underline the verb or verb phrase in each sentence.

1. The first American schools were held in homes.
2. Who invented the jet engine?
3. The *New England Primer* was the earliest United States textbook.
4. John Philip Sousa was a bandmaster and composer.
5. Who built the first motorcycle?
6. My friends will arrive on Saturday afternoon.
7. What was the final score?
8. Ryan has made this unusual birdhouse.
9. The waves covered the beach with many shells.
10. I have ridden on a motor scooter.
11. The artist is molding clay.
12. Beverly and her friends spent last summer in the mountains.
13. The names of the new employees are posted by the supervisor.
14. Paul has found a new hat.
15. She is going to the store.
16. We have trimmed the hedges.
17. The United States exports many kinds of food.
18. My friend is reading a book about World War I.
19. Jane Addams helped many foreign-born people in Chicago, Illinois.
20. Oil was discovered in many parts of North America.
21. Jenny Lind was called the Swedish Nightingale.
22. We are planning a car trip to Miami, Florida.
23. That dog has howled for two hours.
24. Our guests have arrived.
25. I have written letters to several companies.
26. I can name two important cities in that country.
27. The hummingbird received its name because of the sound of its wings.
28. Jan's poem was printed in the newspaper.
29. Charles and Adam are working at the hamburger stand.
30. This table was painted recently.

Gerunds and Gerund Phrases

A **gerund** is the present participle of a verb form ending in –ing that is used as a noun.

A gerund may be a subject, a direct object, or an object of a preposition.

> Examples: **Exercising** is vital to good health. (subject)
>
> Tanya enjoys **exercising**. (direct object)
>
> I have thought about **exercising**. (object of preposition)

A **gerund phrase** consists of a gerund and all the words related to the gerund.

> Examples: **Packing for our trip** was fun.
>
> Mom encourages **careful packing of essentials**.

Underline each gerund.

1. That tribe was successful at planting, hunting, and fishing.
2. Swimming is one of Cassandra's favorite pastimes.
3. We like kayaking and canoeing.
4. Writing is a skill that is required for many jobs.
5. We give a lot of our free time to hiking.
6. Jason taught us the rules of boating.

Underline each gerund phrase and circle the gerund.

7. They always liked living on the farm.
8. Airplanes are used in fighting forest fires.
9. Landing an airplane requires skill.
10. Climbing Pikes Peak is quite an experience.
11. The moaning of the wind through the pines lulled me to sleep.
12. The dog's barking awakened everyone in the house.
13. Keeping his temper is difficult for John.
14. Sue objected to our hanging the picture in this room.
15. The comedian encourages laughing out loud.
16. Being treasurer of this club is a responsibility.
17. Making a speech makes me nervous.
18. Winning this game will place our soccer team first in the league.
19. It was my first attempt at pitching horseshoes.
20. Rapid eating will make digestion difficult.
21. Playing golf is a favorite pastime in many countries.
22. Planning a party requires much thought.
23. The howling of the coyotes disturbed our sleep.

Infinitives and Infinitive Phrases

An **infinitive** is the base form of a verb, commonly preceded by <u>to</u>.

An infinitive may be used as a noun, an adjective, or an adverb.

    Examples: Rachel wants **to dance**. (noun)

    That is the movie **to see**. (adjective)

    She came here **to study**. (adverb)

An **infinitive phrase** consists of an infinitive and all the words related to the infinitive.

    Examples: To win the championship was their goal.

    She found the courage **to speak the truth**.

    Tim called home **to talk to his parents**.

Underline each infinitive.

1. The baby quickly learned to stand and to walk.

2. We will soon be ready to eat.

3. Reggie taught me to dance, but it wasn't easy.

4. Do you have the energy to clean?

5. Everyone on the committee has a job to do.

6. To dream can be very inspiring.

Underline each infinitive phrase and circle the infinitive.

7. I want to go home before dark.

8. Do you want to listen to the song again?

9. I prepared the salad to serve for lunch.

10. To shoot firecrackers in the city limits is against the law here.

11. I like to walk in the country.

12. Gradually people learned to use fire and to make tools.

13. I need to get a new coat.

14. We plan to make the trip in four hours.

15. Jack, try to be on time in the morning.

16. Anthony plans to travel in Canada during August.

17. We were taught to rise early.

18. We were hoping to see you at the reunion.

19. Pay one fee to enter the amusement park.

20. Jennifer, I forgot to mail your package.

21. To cook this turkey will require several hours.

Participles and Participial Phrases

A **participle** is a verb form that may be used as an adjective. Present participles end in –ing, and most past participles end in –d or –ed.

    Examples: A **dripping** faucet can be a nuisance. **Wilted** flowers were removed from the vase.

A **participial phrase** consists of a participle and all the words related to the participle.

    Examples: Living far from the city, I developed a love for nature. The fruits **displayed at the stand** are colorful.

Underline each participle.

1. The scampering cat ran to the nearest tree.
2. A team of deep-sea divers discovered the buried treasure.
3. The dedicated artist worked patiently.
4. Ironed shirts were stacked neatly at the cleaners.
5. Biting insects hovered over our campsite at night.
6. The child ran to his loving father, who comforted him.

Underline each participial phrase and circle the participle.

7. The chart showing sales figures is very helpful.
8. We saw the thunderstorm advancing across the plains.
9. His foot, struck by the falling timbers, was injured.
10. People preparing for a career in aviation should master mathematics.
11. We drove slowly, enjoying every minute of the drive.
12. Onions are among the largest vegetable crops produced in the United States.
13. The truck, burdened with its load, traveled slowly over the rough road.
14. Jan, thinking about her new job, was very happy.
15. Several passengers injured in the accident were brought to the hospital.
16. The fire, fanned by the high winds, threatened the entire area.
17. The man playing the trombone is my brother.
18. Balloons lifting weather instruments are released daily by many weather stations.
19. The people standing near the fence should form a second line.
20. Carefully looking through the catalog, Earl found a Cajun cookbook.
21. We saw a group of riders steadily galloping over the knoll.
22. Cheered by the crowd, the Special Olympics team took a bow.
23. The topic addressed in your paper caught my interest.
24. Encouraged by her boss's words, Gigi continued with the project.
25. Anyone planning to attend the play should leave early.
26. Walking hand in hand, the couple took in the scenery.

65

Absolute Phrases

> An **absolute phrase** consists of (1) a participle or participial phrase, (2) a noun or pronoun that the participle or participial phrase modifies, and (3) any other modifiers of that noun or pronoun. The entire absolute phrase is used to modify an independent clause.
>
> **Examples: Class ended**, we all headed for the assembly hall. **Winter having come early**, we were unprepared for the blizzard.

Underline the absolute phrase in each sentence.

1. The tree being the oldest one in the county, the commissioners passed a law to protect it.
2. The car loaded with suitcases, our vacation was about to begin.
3. Her bicycle having finally been repaired, Teresa went for a long ride.
4. Terrence said that, the weather being so pleasant, he would prefer to go for a hike.
5. Wearily, the explorer trudged through the snow, his loyal dog keeping pace at his side.
6. Bags packed, the whole family headed for the airport.
7. The marching band took the field, instruments raised proudly.
8. Hilda stood on the steps, her arms crossed in a show of defiance.
9. The day being so chilly and rainy, we decided to stay indoors.
10. The clock striking the hour of noon, I thought I'd go for a brisk walk.
11. My feet having become tingly from the cold, I decided to go back inside.
12. They crossed the stream, the water bubbling around the rocks.
13. Then Jill opened the front door, her new puppy straining at the leash.
14. The hike began beautifully, leaves crunching beneath our feet.
15. The team having boarded the bus, the driver started the engine.
16. Polly relaxed by the fire, her hot chocolate steaming deliciously.
17. The music having finished, Jerry and Eileen walked slowly off the dance floor.
18. All the guests having taken their seats, dinner was served.
19. The actors, their costumes having been changed, rushed back onto the stage.
20. The rearview mirror having been checked, Clara backed out of the driveway.
21. The house was put up for sale, bushes pruned to perfection.
22. The pickles having been jarred, it was time for a well-deserved break.
23. Headlights beaming, the truck barreled down the highway.
24. The news story having been posted online, almost everyone knew what had happened.
25. Julie studied late into the night, her brain working to retain all the details.
26. His backpack being torn, Harry looked for a replacement at the gear store.
27. The tree looked sad, its leaves having fallen almost overnight.
28. Jasper, his hands trembling, picked up the injured bird.

Mood

Mood is a form of the verb that shows the manner of doing or being. There are five types of mood: **indicative**, **interrogative**, **imperative**, **conditional**, and **subjunctive**.

Indicative mood states a fact.

> **Example:** Ben **visited** on Friday.

Interrogative mood asks a question.

> **Example:** How many people **went** to the meeting?

Imperative mood expresses a command or request.

> **Examples:** Ask no more questions. Let's **start** immediately.

Conditional mood states a condition that must be present for something else to happen.

> **Examples:** If you **trust** me, we will be successful. The players will be injured if they **do** not **wear** their helmets.

Subjunctive mood indicates a suggestion, a necessity, a wish, or a condition that is contrary to fact.

> **Example:** It is essential that you **store** the kayak properly. (necessity)
> I would help you, if I **were** able. (I am not able.)

Give the mood of each underlined verb.

1. <u>Come</u> here at once. _____

2. I <u>did</u> not <u>see</u> Carolyn. _____

3. If I <u>were</u> not so tired, I would go to a movie. _____

4. <u>Call</u> for him at once. _____

5. Where <u>has</u> Brittany <u>moved</u>? _____

6. The dog only barks if he <u>hears</u> someone outside. _____

7. Please <u>take</u> the turkey out of the oven. _____

8. If the weather <u>is</u> nice, we will go hiking. _____

9. Who <u>invented</u> the sewing machine? _____

10. She will not sing if she still <u>has</u> a cold. _____

11. It is essential that Cleo <u>walk</u> the dog every day. _____

12. My friends <u>painted</u> the entire house. _____

13. Hannah wishes she <u>were</u> able to drive a truck. _____

14. How many people <u>went</u> on the bike ride? _____

15. I suggest that you <u>save</u> some of your money. _____

16. The members of the band <u>sold</u> birthday calendars. _____

17. Pablo greeted me as though I <u>were</u> a stranger. _____

Use the subjunctive mood to express a condition other than what is actually true. The **present subjunctive** expresses a suggestion or necessity.

> **Examples:** We recommend that Marva **run** for student council. (suggestion)
>
> It is essential that she **have** a chance to speak. (necessity)

The **past subjunctive** expresses a condition contrary to fact or expresses a wish.

> **Example:** My friend Leslie teases me as though she **were** my sister. (condition contrary to fact)
>
> Jaime wishes that his mother **were feeling** better. (wish)

Use the conditional mood to state something that might have happened or that could happen.

> **Example:** I would have been happier if I had **won** the chess match.
>
> If the birds **migrate** early, we will miss them.

Underline the effect shown in parentheses that the underlined verb achieves.

18. If I <u>were</u> able to run faster, I could make the team. (condition contrary to fact, suggestion)

19. It is crucial that you <u>check</u> the smoke detectors. (necessity, condition contrary to fact)

20. The little boy wished he <u>were</u> a superhero. (wish, necessity)

21. If we <u>go</u> to dinner first, we may be late for the movie. (something that might happen, condition contrary to fact)

22. Jan recommended that the manager <u>talk</u> to the employee. (wish, suggestion)

23. If I <u>were</u> Christopher, I would be proud of that project. (condition contrary to fact, something that might happen)

24. It is essential that you <u>remain</u> calm. (wish, necessity)

25. The car will run better if you <u>take</u> good care of it. (suggestion, something that might happen)

26. I wish I <u>were</u> on a Caribbean island. (something that might happen, wish)

Complete the sentence using the mood shown in parentheses.

27. Willis insisted that every employee _____ to the picnic. (present subjunctive of <u>invite</u>)

28. I wish I _____ a better singer. (past subjunctive of <u>be</u>)

29. If you _____ to join the league, sign up early. (conditional of <u>want</u>)

30. If she _____ more careful, she would make fewer mistakes. (past subjunctive of <u>be</u>)

31. We will not go to the festival unless the rain _____. (conditional of <u>stop</u>)

32. Myra suggested that we _____ our umbrellas. (present subjunctive of <u>take</u>)

33. More people would attend if there _____ more parking available. (past subjunctive of <u>be</u>)

34. If the flowers _____ dead, then throw them out. (conditional of <u>be</u>)

68

Transitive and Intransitive Verbs

There are two kinds of action verbs: **transitive** and **intransitive**.

A transitive verb has a direct object.

    Example: Jeffrey **painted** the house.

                           D.O.

An intransitive verb does not need an object to complete its meaning.

    Examples: The sun **rises** in the east. She **walks** quickly.

Underline the verb in each sentence. Then write <u>T</u> for transitive or <u>I</u> for intransitive.

_____ 1. Kristina joined the health club in March.

_____ 2. She wanted the exercise to help her stay healthy.

_____ 3. Kristina exercised every day after work.

_____ 4. She and her friend Nancy walked to the health club.

_____ 5. They worked out together.

_____ 6. Nancy preferred the treadmill.

_____ 7. Kristina liked aerobics and running.

_____ 8. Sometimes they switched activities.

_____ 9. Nancy took an aerobics class.

_____ 10. Kristina used the treadmill.

_____ 11. Occasionally they swam in the pool.

_____ 12. Nancy knew more swimming styles than Kristina.

_____ 13. But Kristina had more fun.

_____ 14. She just splashed around in the water.

Underline the transitive verb and circle the direct object in each sentence.

15. Carlos walked Tiny every day.

16. Tiny usually pulled Carlos along.

17. Carlos washed Tiny every other week.

18. Tiny loved water.

19. He splashed Carlos whenever he could.

20. Tiny also loved rawhide bones.

21. He chewed the bones until they were gone.

22. Carlos found Tiny when Tiny was just a puppy.

Active and Passive Voice

Voice refers to the relation of the subject to its verb.
In the **active voice**, the subject acts.

> **Example: I painted** the house.

In the **passive voice**, the subject receives the action.

> **Example:** The house **was painted** by me.

Use the active voice to create a forceful, direct effect.

> **Example:** Maggie **admired** the wood carving. (more direct than passive voice would be)

Use the passive voice when you want to emphasize the receiver of the action, or when you do not know, or do not want to reveal, the performer of the action.

> **Examples:** Liona **was hit** by a baseball. (emphasizes receiver of action)
>
> A special gift **has been hidden** in your room. (performer of action not revealed)
>
> A box of kittens **was left** at the shelter. (performer of action not known)

Write A if the sentence is in the active voice and P if it is in the passive voice.

_____   1. Marty applied for a job in an electronics store.

_____   2. The application was turned in last week.

_____   3. The store's manager reads every application.

_____   4. Then the applicants are interviewed.

_____   5. Marty was interviewed on Monday.

If a sentence would be better in the active voice, rewrite it in the active voice. If the passive-voice sentence has the right effect, write C and explain why.

6. Janice was told by the doctor to rest.

_____

7. At first, Alfredo was puzzled by the math problem.

_____

8. The trapeze artist was watched closely by the crowd.

_____

9. A bouquet of flowers was selected by Nahele.

_____

10. Michael was temporarily blinded by the sun.

_____

Shifts in Voice and Mood

Use the active or passive voice consistently. Avoid unnecessary shifts from one voice to the other.

Example: Giorgio has practiced his guitar, and now many songs can be played by him. (shifts from active to passive)

Corrected: Giorgio has practiced his guitar, and now he can play many songs. (both verbs in active voice)

Example: The date has been set, and they have sent the invitations. (shifts from passive to active)

Corrected: The date **has been set**, and the invitations **have been sent**. (both verbs in passive voice)

Rewrite each sentence to make the voice consistent.

1. Jessica started playing tennis again, and some new shots are being learned by her.

_____

2. A bear's head had been carved, but the sculptor was not pleased with it.

_____

3. He fired the pot again after the glaze had been applied.

_____

Avoid unnecessary shifts from one mood to another.

Example: Clean the garage, and then you should finish your homework. (shifts from imperative mood to indicative mood)

Corrected: Clean the garage, and then **finish** your homework. (both verbs in imperative)

Example: If she were better prepared, she will be able to help us. (shifts from subjunctive mood to indicative mood)

Corrected: If she **were** better prepared, she **would** be able to help us. (stays in subjunctive)

Rewrite each sentence to make the mood consistent.

4. If Miguel were less tired, he will go to the festival

_____

5. Proofread your paper, and then it is good to correct all your errors.

_____

6. It is critical that he find the leak and fixes it.

_____

Subject-Verb Agreement

A verb agrees with its subject in number. Singular subjects take singular verbs, and plural subjects take plural verbs.

Examples: The **ocean roars** in the distance.

The **dancers practice** after school.

The first helping verb in a verb phrase agrees with the subject.

Examples: Latrice has been studying Arabic.

Her **brothers have** been studying Arabic, too.

The number of a subject is not changed by a prepositional phrase that follows the subject.

Examples: The smallest **puppy** of the **three** is sleeping.

These **shades** of **blue** are my favorite colors.

When the subject follows the verb, the subject and verb must still agree.

Examples: Here **is** your **ticket**. Where **are** the **tickets**? Where**'s** your **ticket**?

Identify each subject and verb pair as singular or plural. Write <u>S</u> for singular or <u>P</u> for plural.

_____ 1. socks match

_____ 2. lightning crackles

_____ 3. leaves rustle

_____ 4. mosquitoes buzz

_____ 5. Lyle babysits

_____ 6. bands march

_____ 7. Alexis knits

_____ 8. they listen

_____ 9. singer practices

_____ 10. horses gallop

Underline the correct verb.

11. Firefighters (risks, risk) their lives to save others.

12. (Is, Are) Mandy going to the film festival?

13. At the science fair, the winner (receives, receive) a savings bond.

14. The mayor (has, have) made the announcement.

15. Songs about love often (makes, make) me cry.

16. (Does, Do) the girls go swimming often?

17. There (is, are) the plates for the picnic.

18. Each Saturday, club members (picks, pick) up litter in the park.

19. The jar of lima beans (was, were) stored in the pantry.

20. Strong winds (was, were) whistling through the old house.

21. The students in the karate class (watches, watch) the demonstrations carefully.

22. The birthday cards on the table (is, are) for Manuel.

23. My mother (prefers, prefer) a good book to a good movie.

A compound subject joined by <u>and</u> usually takes a plural verb.

Examples: Mr. Lewis and **Mrs. Kirk** teach science.

Two singular subjects joined by <u>or</u> or <u>nor</u> take a singular verb. When a singular subject and a plural subject are joined by <u>or</u> or <u>nor</u>, the verb agrees with the subject nearer to the verb.

Examples: Neither **Marco** nor **Raymond** has ever seen an opera.

A soft **blanket** or warm **booties make** a good gift for a baby.

Underline the correct verb.

24. The blanket and the robe (has, have) Navajo designs.
25. Wind, hail, and rain (is, are) predicted for Thursday.
26. Rice or potatoes (comes, come) with the grilled chicken.
27. A desk and a bookcase (was, were) moved into Ella's room.
28. Neither North Carolina nor Illinois (borders, border) Texas.
29. Flowers or a colorful picture (makes, make) a room cheerful.
30. A truck and a car with a trailer (was, were) stalled on the highway.
31. Either the story or the poem (is, are) by Langston Hughes.
32. Both my brother and my sister (draws, draw) well.
33. Mavis and her aunt (walks, walk) every day.

These indefinite pronouns are singular: <u>anybody</u>, <u>anyone</u>, <u>each</u>, <u>either</u>, <u>everybody</u>, <u>everyone</u>, <u>neither</u>, <u>nobody</u>, <u>no one</u>, <u>one</u>, <u>somebody</u>, and <u>someone</u>.

Example: Everyone who **enjoys** sports **likes** this program.

These indefinite pronouns are plural: <u>both</u>, <u>few</u>, <u>many</u>, <u>several</u>.

Example: Many of the recipes **are** difficult.

The indefinite pronouns <u>all</u>, <u>any</u>, <u>most</u>, <u>none</u>, and <u>some</u> are singular when they refer to singular words and plural when they refer to plural words.

Examples: Most of the book **is** interesting. **Most** of the students **are** here.

Underline the correct verb.

34. Neither of the teams (is, are) on the field.
35. Everybody in Lee's family (enjoys, enjoy) bird's-nest soup.
36. Several of the people in the crowd (is, are) waving pennants.
37. All of the jewels (is, are) in the safe.
38. Either of those salads (tastes, taste) delicious.
39. Most of the balloons (has, have) long strings.
40. Each of those songs (was, were) written by Shawn Colvin.

Pronouns

A **pronoun** is a word used in place of a noun.

A **personal pronoun** is chosen based on the way it is used in the sentence.

A **subjective pronoun** is used in the subject of a sentence and after a linking verb.

> **Examples: He** is a chemist. The chemist is **he**.

An **objective pronoun** is used after an action verb or a preposition.

> **Examples:** Jan gave **me** the gift. Jan gave the gift to **me**.

A **possessive pronoun** is used to show ownership of something.

> **Examples:** The new car is **ours**. That is **our** car.

Underline each pronoun.

1. Brian, do you have my ticket to the play?
2. Just between you and me, I want to go with them.
3. Carol, will you help me carry our trunk?
4. May I go with you?
5. We saw him standing in line to go to a movie.
6. Just be sure to find Carol and me.
7. We will be ready when they come for us.
8. She sent this box of frozen steaks to Andrea and me.
9. She asked you and me to be on her bowling team.
10. We saw them go into the building on the corner.
11. Last week we sent flowers to our sick friend.
12. He must choose their dinner.
13. She is my English instructor.
14. They have never invited us to go with them.
15. The first-place winner is she.
16. Can he compete against you?
17. She made the dinner for us.
18. Liz and I are going on vacation in June.
19. Where is your umbrella?
20. Sharon gave me a book to read.
21. Do you know where our cottage is?
22. If I lend you my car, will you take care of it?
23. I gave him my word that we would visit her.
24. When they saw us fishing, Bob and Diane changed their clothes.

Demonstrative, Indefinite, and Intensive Pronouns

A **demonstrative pronoun** is used to point out a specific person or thing.

This and that are used in place of singular nouns. This refers to a person or thing nearby, and that refers to a person or thing farther away.

> **Examples: This** is mine. **That** is the right one.

These and those are used in place of plural nouns. These points to persons or things nearby, and those points to persons or things farther away.

> **Examples: These** are the best ones. **Those** don't look ripe.

Underline each demonstrative pronoun.

1. Those are the books I lost.
2. That is where Anne lives.
3. I'm not sure these are my scissors.
4. This is my pen; that is Pam's book.
5. I think those are interesting books.

6. This is Gretchen's timecard.
7. Was that your first mistake?
8. Give these to your friend.
9. These are Stephanie's shoes.
10. I think that was just a rumor.

An **indefinite pronoun** does not refer to a specific person or thing.

> **Examples: Many** are called, but **few** are chosen. **Everyone** is ready. I like **several** of the items on the menu.

Underline each indefinite pronoun.

11. Both of them worked hard.
12. Let each help decorate.
13. Several have called about the job.
14. Unfortunately, some never learn.
15. Some of the students asked for pens.

16. I think someone forgot his sweater.
17. Everyone was delighted about the party.
18. He thinks that each is right.
19. Has anyone seen my wallet?
20. Everybody arrived late.

An **intensive pronoun** emphasizes a noun or another pronoun.

> **Examples:** The students **themselves** painted the mural. He coolly suggested that I return it **myself**.

Underline each intensive pronoun.

21. I myself have never been to Hong Kong.
22. They themselves performed the pantomime.
23. Craig finished the puzzle himself.

24. I think Terry designed the costume herself.
25. Andy baked the bread himself, with some help.
26. The players themselves honored the coach.

75

Antecedents

An **antecedent** is the word to which a pronoun refers.

    Example: Stars are lovely when **they** shine.

A pronoun must agree with its antecedent in **gender** (**masculine**, **feminine**, or **neuter**) and **number** (**singular** or **plural**).

    Examples: Susan helped **her** friend. The **people** went in **their** cars.

If the antecedent is a singular indefinite pronoun, use both a masculine and a feminine pronoun to refer to it.

    Example: Someone lost **his or her** dog.

Underline the correct pronoun or pronouns and circle the antecedent. The first one has been done for you.

1. (Everyone) should work hard at (their, <u>his or her</u>) job.
2. Each of the children willingly did (his or her, their) share of the camp duties.
3. Sophia gave me (her, their) coat to wear.
4. I took (my, our) friend to the ceremony.
5. All members were asked to bring (his or her, their) contributions today.
6. The women have had (her, their) vacation.
7. Someone has left (her or his, their) automobile across the driveway.
8. If each does (his or her, their) best, our chorus will win.
9. Would you tell Joanne that (her, his) soup is ready?
10. Every woman did (her, their) best to make the program a success.
11. Never judge anyone entirely by (his or her, their) looks.
12. Each student should do (his or her, their) own work.
13. I lost (my, our) favorite earring at the dance.
14. Each woman takes (her, their) own equipment on the camping trip.
15. Each one has a right to (his or her, their) own opinion in this matter.
16. (His, Her) sense of humor is what I like best about Joseph.
17. Some man has left (his, their) raincoat.
18. The two waiters dropped (his, their) trays when they bumped into each other.
19. Has each student received (his or her, their) report card?
20. Every person is expected to do (her or his, their) best.
21. We knew that every man at the meeting expressed (his, their) opinion.
22. Every woman furnishes (her, their) own transportation.
23. Jeff and Tom found (his, their) cabin in the dark.
24. Cliff brings his dog every time (he, she) visits.

Common Problems with Pronouns

A **pronoun** should refer clearly to its **antecedent**. Avoid **ambiguous references**, which occur when a pronoun refers to either of two antecedents.

    Example: Lois called Rosa while **she** was in Miami.

    Corrected: While Lois was in Miami, she called Rosa.

Avoid **unclear references**, which occur when a pronoun such as <u>it</u>, <u>this</u>, <u>that</u>, <u>which</u>, <u>they</u>, or <u>you</u> does not have a specific, definite antecedent that is stated in the sentence.

    Example: Josie sang beautifully. **This** impressed the audience.

    Corrected: Josie impressed the audience by singing beautifully.

    Example: I want to be a playwright, but **it** isn't offered at my school.

    Corrected: I want to be a playwright, but a course in playwrighting isn't offered at my school.

    Example: In Mexico City, **they** have a huge festival on May 5.

    Corrected: Mexico City has a huge festival on May 5.

Rewrite each sentence to correct the ambiguous or unclear pronoun reference.

1. In the article it calls the mayor's plan unwise.

_____

2. Jen was waiting for Heidi outside her house.

_____

3. Dee writes stories, and she hopes to make it her career.

_____

When using pronouns, avoid shifts in person.

    Example: **They** learned that with practice **you** can improve. (shift from third person to second person)

    Corrected: **They** learned that with practice **they** can improve. (both pronouns in third person)

Avoid shifts in number from the antecedent to the pronoun.

    Example: A **player** should listen carefully to **their** coach. (shift from singular to plural)

    Corrected: A player should listen carefully to **his or her** coach.

    Players should listen carefully to **their** coach.

Rewrite each sentence to correct the shift in person or number.

4. They have found that hard work helps you achieve more.

_____

5. A student should follow their teacher's instructions carefully.

_____

Relative Pronouns

A **relative pronoun** is a pronoun that can introduce a dependent clause. The relative pronouns are who, whom, whose (referring to persons); which (referring to things); and that (referring to persons or things).

A **dependent clause**, when introduced by a relative pronoun, serves as an adjective. It modifies a noun or pronoun in the main clause. The word modified is also the antecedent of the relative pronoun.

Examples: Tom knows the author **whose** articles we read in class. The family for **whom** I work is from Canada. The movie **that** won the prize is playing.

Underline each relative pronoun and circle its antecedent. The first one has been done for you.

1. The letter that was published in our daily paper was very long.
2. It was Karen who sang the most difficult song.
3. Robert Burns, who wrote "My Heart's in the Highlands," was Scottish.
4. It was Sylvia who wanted Zach's address.
5. The shop that was filled with video games is going out of business.
6. My parents live in a New England farmhouse that was built many years ago.
7. This is the pearl that is so valuable.
8. The bridge, which is made of wood, was built two hundred years ago.
9. Did you see the animal that ran across the road?
10. Good roads have opened up many regions that were formerly impassable.
11. For our Thanksgiving dinner, we had a turkey that weighed twenty pounds.
12. This story, which was written by Eudora Welty, is most interesting.
13. Anna is a person whom you can trust.
14. We ate the delicious hamburgers that Andrew had prepared.
15. Food that is eaten in pleasant surroundings is usually digested easily.
16. This is the first painting that I did.
17. The sweater that you want is too expensive.
18. She is the one whom we watched at the track meet.
19. The only money that they spent was for food.
20. Your friend is one person who is inconsiderate.
21. A rare animal that lives in our city zoo was featured on the evening news.
22. Heather is one of the guests whom I invited.
23. Is this the file for which you've been searching?
24. Leonardo da Vinci is the artist whose work they most admire.
25. The science museum is an attraction that is visited by many tourists.
26. Charles Dickens is a writer whom I've read extensively.

Using *Who* and *Whom*

Use <u>who</u> as a subjective pronoun.

Example: Who came to the party?

Use <u>whom</u> as an objective pronoun.

Example: Whom did the nurse help?

By rearranging the sentence to read <u>The nurse did help</u> **whom?**, you can see that <u>whom</u> follows the verb and is the object of the verb. It can also be the object of a preposition.

Example: To **whom** did you wish to speak?

Complete each sentence with <u>Who</u> or <u>Whom</u>.

1. _____ is that man?

2. _____ made the first moon landing?

3. _____ would you choose as the winner?

4. _____ is your best friend?

5. _____ gets the reward?

6. _____ will be staying with you this summer?

7. _____ did the instructor invite to speak to the class?

8. _____ did you see at the park?

9. _____ will you contact at headquarters?

10. _____ will you write about?

11. _____ is available to babysit for me on Saturday?

12. _____ did you drive to the store?

13. _____ would like to travel to Hawaii next summer?

14. _____ raced in the track meet?

15. _____ did they meet at the airport?

16. _____ are your three favorite authors?

17. _____ owns that new blue car?

18. _____ did you help last week?

19. _____ wrote that clever poem?

20. _____ will you ask to help you move?

21. _____ brought that salad?

Adjectives

An **adjective** is a word that modifies a noun or a pronoun.
> **Example:** He likes **chocolate** cookies.

Adjectives usually tell **what kind**, **which one**, or **how many**.
> **Examples: bright** penny, **these** oranges, **twelve** classmates

A **proper adjective** is an adjective that is formed from a proper noun.
It always begins with a capital letter.
> **Examples: Asian** continent, **English** language

The articles <u>a</u>, <u>an</u>, and <u>the</u> are called **limiting adjectives**.

Write three adjectives to describe each noun.

1. mountains _____ _____ _____
2. weather _____ _____ _____
3. journey _____ _____ _____
4. classroom _____ _____ _____
5. book _____ _____ _____

Underline each adjective.

6. This old chair is comfortable.
7. We have read a funny story recently.
8. This heavy traffic creates many dangerous situations.
9. The eager sailors collected odd souvenirs at every port.
10. The tired, thirsty soldiers marched on.
11. This is my favorite book.
12. The solitary guard walked along the lonely beach.
13. We sat in the sixth row.
14. These damp matches will not strike.
15. Dan made French toast for breakfast.
16. Will you light those candles, please?
17. A red bird chirped loudly in the tall tree.
18. The heavy elephant sat down slowly.
19. A tour bus stopped at the cove.
20. The gorgeous model wore Italian leather.
21. We ate fresh seafood in Maine.
22. Do you like mashed or baked potatoes?
23. She served Chinese food for dinner.

Demonstrative Adjectives

A **demonstrative adjective** is one that points out a specific person or thing.

This and that modify singular nouns. This points to a person or thing nearby, and that points to a person or thing farther away.

    Examples: This movie is my favorite. **That** sign is difficult to see.

These and those modify plural nouns. These points to persons or things nearby, and those points to persons or things farther away.

    Examples: These ribbons are the most colorful. **Those** towels need to be folded.

The word them is a pronoun. Never use it to describe a noun.

Underline the correct demonstrative adjective.

1. Move (those, them) plants inside since it may freeze tonight.
2. (These, That) box in front of me is too heavy to lift.
3. Who brought us (those, them) delicious cookies?
4. Look at (those, them) playful kittens.
5. (That, Those) kind of friend is appreciated.
6. (Those, Them) pictures are beautiful.
7. What are (those, them) sounds I hear?
8. Did you ever meet (those, them) people?
9. We have just posted (these, them) photographs online.
10. Do you know any of (those, them) young people?
11. May we take some of (these, them) folders?
12. I have been looking over (these, them) magazines.
13. Do not eat too many of (those, them) peaches.
14. I do not like (this, these) kind of syrup.
15. (Those, Them) people should be served next.
16. Jimmy, please send (those, them) emails by tomorrow.
17. Look at (those, them) posters I made!
18. (This, That) suburb is fifty miles away.
19. (These, Them) antique coins are valuable.
20. Look at (those, that) soccer players hustle!
21. Jose, may we see (those, them) photographs?
22. Please return (that, these) library books.
23. (These, Them) clothes need to be washed.
24. Please hand me (that, those) plates.
25. (Those, Them) cookies have nuts in them.

Comparing with Adjectives

An adjective has three degrees of comparison: **positive**, **comparative**, and **superlative**.

The simple form of the adjective is called the **positive** degree.

>   **Example:** Ian is **short**.

When two people or things are being compared, the **comparative** degree is used.

>   **Example:** Ian is **shorter** than Lee.

When three or more people or things are being compared, the **superlative** degree is used.

>   **Example:** Ian is the **shortest** person in the group.

For all adjectives of one syllable and a few adjectives of two syllables, add -**er** to form the comparative degree and -**est** to form the superlative degree.

>   **Example:** smart — smarter — smartest

For some adjectives of two syllables and all adjectives of three or more syllables, use <u>more</u> or <u>less</u> to form the comparative and <u>most</u> or <u>least</u> to form the superlative.

>   **Examples:** This test is **more** difficult than I expected. Carol is the **most** generous of all. Kate is **less** talkative than Tom. Mary is the **least** talkative of all.

Complete each sentence with the correct degree of comparison of the adjective given in parentheses. Some of the forms are irregular.

1. (changeable)   The weather seems ____more changeable____ this year than last.

2. (faithful)   I think the dog is the ____most faithful____ of all animals.

3. (agreeable)   Is James ____more agreeable____ than Sam?

4. (busy)   Theresa is the ____busiest____ person in the office.

5. (long)   Which is the ____longer____ river, the Mississippi or the Amazon?

6. (lovely)   I think the rose is the ____loveliest____ of all flowers.

7. (fresh)   Show me the ____freshest____ cookies in the store.

8. (high)   Which of the two mountains is ____higher____?

9. (enjoyable)   Which is the ____most enjoyable____, television or the movies?

10. (reckless)   That person is the ____most reckless____ driver in town.

11. (young)   Of all the players, Maria is the ____youngest____.

12. (tall)   Alberto is the ____tallest____ of the three men.

13. (difficult)   Isn't the seventh problem ____more difficult____ than the eighth?

14. (quiet)   We have found the ____a most quiet____ spot in the park.

Adverbs

An **adverb** is a word that modifies a verb, an adjective, or another adverb.
Examples: The rain poured **steadily**. His memories were **extremely** vivid. She responded **very** quickly.

An adverb usually tells **how**, **when**, **where**, or **how often**.
Many adverbs end in -<u>ly</u>.

Underline each adverb.

1. The person read slowly but clearly and expressively.
2. Adam, you are driving too recklessly.
3. The airplane started moving slowly but quickly gained speed.
4. I spoke too harshly to my friends.
5. How did all of you get here?
6. I looked everywhere for my pen.
7. The man stopped suddenly and quickly turned around.
8. Stacy read that poem too rapidly.
9. Janice plays the guitar well.
10. The child was sleeping soundly.
11. The car was running noisily.
12. We returned early.
13. Those trees were severely damaged in the fire.
14. Jack ran quickly, but steadily, in the race.

Write two adverbs that could be used to modify each verb.

15. read _____   _____
16. think _____   _____
17. walk _____   _____
18. eat _____   _____
19. sing _____   _____
20. speak _____   _____
21. dive _____   _____
22. study _____   _____
23. write _____   _____
24. look _____   _____

Comparing with Adverbs

An **adverb** has three degrees of comparion: **positive**, **comparative**, and **superlative**.

The simple form of the adverb is called the **positive** degree.

    Example: Kathy ran **fast** in the race.

When two actions are being compared, the **comparative** degree is used.

    Example: Amy ran **faster** than Kathy.

When three or more actions are being compared, the **superlative** degree is used.

    Example: Maureen ran the **fastest** of all.

Use -**er** to form the comparative degree and use -**est** to form the superlative degree of one-syllable adverbs.

Use **more** or **most** with longer adverbs and with adverbs that end in -**ly**.

    Examples: Louisa ran **more energetically** than Bob. Ms. Baker ran the **most energetically** of all the runners.

Underline the adverb that best completes each sentence.

1. Mark arrived (sooner, soonest) than Greg.

2. Tony arrived the (sooner, soonest) of all.

3. They had to work very (hard, harder, hardest).

4. Tony painted (more, most) carefully than Mark.

5. Mark worked (faster, fastest) than Greg, so Mark painted the walls.

6. Lauren worked the (more, most) carefully of all.

Complete each sentence with the proper form of the adverb in parentheses.

7. (fast)   Jason wanted to run the _____ at our school.

8. (fast)   Juan could run _____ than Jason.

9. (seriously)   Jason trained _____ than he had before.

10. (frequently)   Jason is on the track _____ of all the runners.

11. (quickly)   Jason ran the sprint _____ than he did yesterday.

12. (promptly)   Jason arrives for practice _____ of anyone on the team.

13. (promptly)   He even arrives _____ than the coach!

14. (eagerly)   Juan does warm-up exercises _____ of all the runners.

15. (carefully)   Who concentrates _____ on his timing, Juan or Jason?

16. (hard)   The coach congratulates Jason on being the runner who works the _____.

Adjectives and Adverbs

Underline the correct word.

1. Always drive very (careful, **carefully**).

2. The lake seems (**calm**, calmly) today.

3. The storm raged (furious, **furiously**).

4. The dog waited (patient, **patiently**) for its owner.

5. Nicole's letters are always (cheerful, **cheerfully**) written.

6. Although our team played (good, **well**), we lost the game.

7. Always answer your mail (prompt, **promptly**).

8. James speaks (respectful, **respectfully**) to everyone.

9. Tara is (**happy**, happily) with her new work.

10. Write this address (legible, **legibly**).

11. The time passed (slow, **slowly**).

12. The robin chirped (happy, **happily**) from its nest.

13. We were (**sure**, surely) glad to hear from him.

14. Rebecca tries to do her work (good, **well**).

15. I think Brenda will (easy, **easily**) win that contest.

16. We had to talk (loud, **loudly**) to be heard.

17. Yesterday the sun shone (bright, **brightly**) all day.

18. He says he sleeps (good, **well**) every night.

19. The elevator went up (quick, **quickly**) to the top floor.

20. The storm began very (sudden, **suddenly**)

21. You did react very (cautious, **cautiously**).

22. Every student should do this work (accurate, **accurately**).

23. Eric rode his bike (furious, **furiously**) to get home on time.

24. The paint on the house is (**new**, newly).

25. The mist fell (steady, **steadily**) all evening.

26. The river looked (**beautiful**, beautifully) in the moonlight.

27. The salesperson always answers questions (courteous, **courteously**).

28. He always does (good, **well**) when selling that product.

29. Ryan can swim (good, **well**).

30. I was (real, **really**) excited about going to San Francisco.

31. I think he talks (foolish, **foolishly**).

32. It seems (**foolish**, foolishly) to me.

33. That bell rang too (loud, **loudly**) for this small room.

34. Our grass seems to grow very (rapid, **rapidly**).

85

Prepositions

A **preposition** is a word that shows the relationship of a noun or a pronoun to another word in the sentence.

Examples: Put the package **on** the table. Place the package **in** the desk.

These are some commonly used prepositions:

about	against	at	between	from	of	through	under
above	among	behind	by	in	on	to	upon
across	around	beside	for	into	over	toward	with

Underline each preposition in the sentences below.

1. The grin on Juan's face was bright and warm.
2. He greeted his cousin from Brazil with a smile and a handshake.
3. They walked through the airport and toward the baggage area.
4. Luis found his bags between two boxes.
5. The two cousins had not seen each other for five years.
6. They could spend hours talking about everything.
7. Juan and Luis got into Juan's truck.
8. Juan drove Luis to Juan's family's ranch.
9. It was a long ride across many hills and fields.
10. Luis rested his head against the seat.
11. Soon they drove over a hill and into a valley.
12. The ranch was located across the Harrison River.
13. The house stood among a group of oak trees.
14. Juan parked the truck beside the driveway.
15. They walked across the driveway and toward the house.
16. Juan's mother, Anita, stood behind the screen door.
17. Juan's family gathered around Luis.
18. Everyone sat on the porch and drank lemonade.
19. "Tell us about our relatives in Brazil," Rosa asked.
20. "You have over twenty cousins in my area," said Luis.
21. "Many of them are still in school."
22. Then everyone went into the house and ate dinner.
23. Juan's family passed the food across the table.
24. "Many of these dishes come from old family recipes," he said.
25. "It is wonderful to be among so many relatives," Luis said.
26. After dinner, everyone went to the living room.
27. Luis showed them photographs of his home in Brazil.

86

Prepositional Phrases

> A **phrase** is a group of closely related words used as a single part of speech but not containing a subject and predicate.
>
> **Example:** The writer **of this novel** is signing autographs.
>
> A **prepositional phrase** is a group of words that begins with a preposition and ends with a noun or pronoun.
>
> **Example:** He took the train **to New York**.
>
> The noun or pronoun in the prepositional phrase is called the **object of the preposition**.
>
> **Example:** He took the train to **New York**.

Put parentheses around each prepositional phrase. Then underline each preposition and circle the object of the preposition. The first one has been done for you.

1. The airplane was flying (above the clouds).
2. We are moving (to North Carolina.)
3. Sandra lives (on the second block.)
4. An old water tower once stood (on that hill.)
5. The car slid (on the wet pavement.)
6. Sealing wax was invented (in the seventeenth century.)
7. Motto rings were first used (by the Romans.)
8. Tungsten, a metal, was discovered (in 1781.)
9. Roses originally came (from Asia.)
10. The ball rolled (into the street.)
11. Do you always keep the puppies (in a pen?)
12. The children climbed (over the fence.)
13. She lives (in Denver, Colorado.)
14. Columbus made three trips (to North America.)
15. They spread the lunch under the shade (of the giant elm tree.)
16. The treasure was found (by a scuba diver.)
17. A squad (of soldiers) marched (behind the tank.)
18. Shall I row (across the stream?)
19. Large airplanes fly (across the nation.)
20. Walter looked (into the sack.)
21. The cat ran (up the pole.)
22. We visited the Alexander Graham Bell Museum (in Nova Scotia.)
23. Many tourists come (to our region.)
24. We spent last summer (in the Adirondack Mountains.)

Prepositional Phrases as Adjectives and Adverbs

A prepositional phrase can be used to describe a noun or a pronoun. Then the prepositional phrase is being used as an **adjective** to tell which one, what kind, or how many.

Example: The bird **in the tree** whistled.

The prepositional phrase <u>in the tree</u> tells **which** bird.

A prepositional phrase can be used to describe a verb. Then the prepositional phrase is being used as an **adverb** to tell how, where, or when.

Example: Charlie ate breakfast **before leaving for school**.

The prepositional phrase <u>before leaving for school</u> tells **when** Charlie ate breakfast.

Underline each prepositional phrase and classify it as adjective or adverb.

1. They went to the ranch. _____

2. The first savings bank was established in France. _____

3. Fall Creek Falls in Tennessee is my home. _____

4. Return all books to the public library. _____

5. Mark lives in an old house. _____

6. Tanya bought a sweater with red trim. _____

7. The birds in the zoo are magnificent. _____

8. Jade is found in Burma. _____

9. I spent the remainder of my money. _____

10. The magician waved a wand over the hat, and a rabbit appeared. _____

11. The diameter of a Sequoia tree trunk can reach ten feet. _____

12. The capital of New York is Albany. _____

13. The narrowest streets are near the docks. _____

14. Our family went to the movie. _____

15. Roald Amundsen discovered the South Pole in 1911. _____

16. The floor in this room is painted black. _____

17. The dead leaves are blowing across the yard. _____

18. A forest of petrified wood has been found. _____

19. The mole's tunnel runs across the lawn. _____

Misplaced and Dangling Modifiers

Avoid using misplaced modifiers. A **misplaced modifier** is a word, phrase, or clause that seems to modify the wrong word or word group.

Example: The students were planning a field trip **in the library**.

Corrected: The students **in the library** were planning a field trip.

Example: I bought a ladder to fix the roof that was sturdy.

Corrected: I bought a ladder **that was sturdy** to fix the roof.

Rewrite each sentence to correct the misplaced modifier.

1. The log fit into the fireplace broken in half.

   _____

2. Martin watched a radiant sunset climbing a hill.

   _____

3. Jolene gave a bird to her brother that has white feathers.

   _____

4. Earl discovered many beetles examining the rosebushes.

   _____

Avoid using dangling modifiers. A **dangling modifier** is a modifying word, phrase, or clause that does not clearly and sensibly modify any word or word group.

Example: Frustrated, most of Mary's paper had to be retyped.

Corrected: Frustrated, Mary had to retype most of her paper.

Example: After turning on the radio, the baby woke up.

Corrected: After I turned on the radio, the baby woke up.

Rewrite each sentence to correct the dangling modifier.

5. Looking back over my shoulder, the team went into a huddle.

   _____

6. To repair an appliance, experience is helpful.

   _____

7. Exhausted, the tent still had to be set up.

   _____

8. When leaving the train, the station is on the right.

   _____

Conjunctions

A **conjunction** is a word used to join words or groups of words.

    Example: Jenna **and** her sister are in Arizona.

These are some commonly used conjunctions:

although	because	how	or	that	when	while
and	but	if	since	so	though	whereas
yet	as	for	nor	than	unless	whether

Some conjunctions are used in pairs. These include <u>either... or</u>, <u>neither... nor</u>, and <u>not only... but also</u>.

Underline each conjunction.

1. He and I are friends.

2. David likes tennis, whereas Jim prefers running.

3. We had to wait because it was raining.

4. We left early, but we missed the train.

5. The show was not only long but also boring.

6. Neither the chairs nor the tables had been dusted.

7. Hail and sleet fell during the storm.

8. Neither Carmen nor Kara was able to attend the meeting.

9. I have neither time nor energy to waste.

10. Bowling and tennis are my favorite sports.

11. Either Dan or Don will bring a portable media player.

12. The people in the car and the people in the van exchanged greetings.

13. Both fruits and vegetables are part of a healthful diet.

14. Although I like to take photographs, I am not a good photographer.

15. Did you see Charles when he visited here?

16. We are packing our bags because our trip begins tomorrow.

17. She cannot concentrate while you are making so much noise.

18. Unless you hurry, you will miss the party.

19. We enjoyed the visit although we were very tired.

20. Both mammals and birds are warm-blooded.

21. She has been practicing, yet she still cannot dance well.

22. Unless you have some objections, I will submit this report.

23. Neither dogs nor cats are allowed in this park.

24. April watered the plants while Luis mowed the lawn.

25. I will see you when you are feeling better.

26. Either Ms. Andretti or Ms. Garcia will teach that course.

Nonstandard Usage

Standard English is the accepted usage and conventions for formal writing and speaking. Always use Standard English in your writing for school. Keep in mind that standard usage can change over time. If you are not sure what the current preferred usage is, consult a style guide such as *Merriam-Webster's Dictionary of English Usage* or *Garner's Modern American Usage*.

Do not use a word such as <u>not</u>, <u>never</u>, <u>hardly</u>, <u>scarcely</u>, <u>seldom</u>, <u>none</u>, or <u>nothing</u> with another negative word. This type of nonstandard usage is called a double negative.

    Example: There wasn't nothing left in the refrigerator.

    Corrected: There was nothing left in the refrigerator.

When forming comparisons, do not use both –er and <u>more</u> or both –est and <u>most</u>. This type of nonstandard usage is called a **double comparison**.

    Example: These enchiladas are more tastier than the tacos.

    Corrected: These enchiladas are tastier than the tacos.

Underline the correct word or words in parentheses.

1. We couldn't see (nothing, anything) through the fog.
2. That's the (most funniest, funniest) story I ever heard!
3. Grandpa seems (wiser, more wiser) than anyone else I know.
4. I don't want (any, no) cereal for breakfast this morning.
5. This is the (oldest, most oldest) covered bridge in the United States.
6. There (wasn't, was) nobody in the house.
7. I don't remember (never, ever) eating a plantain.
8. If the water were (more deeper, deeper), we could dive safely.
9. Do not speak to (anyone, no one) about the surprise party.
10. He (can't, can) hardly reach the top shelf.

Rewrite each sentence to correct the double negative or double comparison.

11. The most strangest noise is coming from behind that door.

_____

12. I don't know none of the people on this bus.

_____

13. We have never had no problems with our car.

_____

14. Joe needs a more shorter board for the birdhouse floor.

_____

Unit 3 Review

Write the part of speech above each underlined word. Use the abbreviations given in the box.

n. noun	*pron.* pronoun	*v.* verb	*adj.* adjective
adv. adverb	*prep.* preposition	*conj.* conjunction	

1. A <u>heavy</u> dust <u>storm</u> <u>rolled</u> <u>across</u> the <u>prairie</u>.

2. This is <u>a</u> <u>nice</u> <u>surprise</u>!

3. The <u>dark</u> <u>clouds</u> <u>slowly</u> <u>gathered</u> in the north.

4. <u>Marlee</u> and <u>I</u> are showing slides <u>of</u> the photographs that <u>we</u> took on our <u>trip</u>.

5. Is the <u>capital</u> <u>of</u> your state <u>built</u> on a <u>river</u>?

6. <u>These</u> shrubs <u>are</u> <u>beautiful</u>.

7. <u>Someone</u> opened the door <u>very</u> <u>cautiously</u> <u>and</u> tiptoed inside.

8. Please <u>handle</u> <u>this</u> <u>extremely</u> fragile china <u>very</u> carefully.

9. <u>The</u> weary <u>people</u> waited <u>for</u> the <u>long</u> <u>parade</u> to start.

10. <u>Large</u> herds of <u>longhorn</u> cattle grazed on <u>these</u> <u>vast</u> plains.

11. <u>We</u> are going <u>to</u> the <u>new</u> <u>mall</u> <u>today</u>, <u>but</u> Sara can't go with us.

12. <u>Floyd</u>, <u>you</u> are eating <u>that</u> food <u>too</u> <u>rapidly</u>.

Write the plural form or the possessive form of the noun in parentheses.

13. (bench) The park _____ need to be painted.

14. (fly) The _____ landed on our picnic lunch.

15. (hero) All of the _____ medals were awarded at the ceremony.

16. (pony) Her _____ saddle has been cleaned and oiled.

17. (watch) My _____ hands have stopped moving.

Underline the appositive or appositive phrase and circle the noun it identifies.

18. We plan to visit Ottawa, the capital of Canada, on our vacation.

19. My older sister Kira is an engineer.

20. We ate a hearty breakfast, pancakes and ham, before going to work.

Underline the correct verb.

21. The members of the chess club (practices, practice) often.

22. Pollution and congestion (result, results) from use of automobiles.

23. Neither Jack nor his brother (is, are) going to the dance.

24. Those chefs (make, makes) delicious food.

25. Few of the students (is, are) familiar with that poet's work.

26. Most of the article (is, are) interesting.

27. Jessica and Glen (plays, play) soccer well.

28. The advice from our teacher usually (proves, prove) helpful.

Underline the verbal in each sentence and write infinitive, participle, or gerund on the line.

_____ **29.** The reason they went to the lake was to fish.

_____ **30.** Skating has become a popular sport.

_____ **31.** The flashing lights warned people of danger.

_____ **32.** Juan's goal is to finish law school.

_____ **33.** The improved detergent cleaned better than the old formula.

Underline the pronoun in parentheses that agrees with the antecedent. Circle the antecedent.

34. Curtis and Erika tutored Mark because (he, they) had missed the review.

35. The office workers had to leave (their, its) building when a fire started.

36. Bob and Andre brought the posters to (them, their) campaign office.

37. My sister collected baskets on (her, their) trip to Mexico.

38. The volunteers accepted donations and gave (it, them) to the charity.

Circle the correct word in parentheses.

39. Please don't give me (any, no) more trouble.

40. Leila found the (most prettiest, prettiest) bracelet at that shop.

41. The toddler (couldn't, could) hardly walk two feet without falling.

42. His new cell phone is (smaller, more smaller) than the old one.

Unit 3: Grammar and Usage
Core Skills Grammar Review

Using What You've Learned

Read the following paragraphs. Then use the paragraphs to complete the items below.

Tibet, which is a remote land in south-central Asia, is often called the Roof of the World or Land of the Snows. Its mountains and plateaus are the highest in the world. The capital of Tibet, Lhasa, is 12,000 feet high.

Tibetans, who are sometimes called the hermit people, follow a simple way of life. They are a short and sturdy people and do heavy physical work. Some are nomads, herders who roam about in the northern uplands of the country. Once a year, the nomads come to the low regions to sell their products and to buy things that they need. They live in tents made of yak hair. A yak is about the size of a small ox and has long hair. Yaks are good companions to the nomads because they can live and work in the high altitudes.

1. Write two appositives from the paragraphs above.

_____

_____

Write four relative pronouns and their antecedents.

2. _____   _____

3. _____   _____

4. _____   _____

5. _____   _____

Write three prepositional phrases.

6. _____

7. _____

8. _____

9. **Write one superlative adjective.** _____

10. **Write one indefinite pronoun.** _____

11. **Write two intransitive verbs.** _____   _____

12. **Write two infinitives.** _____   _____

13. **Write two conjunctions.** _____   _____

Name _____ Date _____

Read the following paragraphs. Then use the paragraphs to complete the items below.

If you were to guess which people were the first to learn to write, would you guess the Egyptians? Experts believe thousands of years ago, around 3100 B.C., Egyptians first began writing. Much of their writing was done to record historical events. Later, writings were used on pyramids to ensure peace for the kings buried in them. The writings were in hieroglyphics, a system of writing based on pictures.

Egyptian pyramids are notable for a number of reasons. The oldest pyramid is called Saqqarah. It was built with hundreds of steps running up to the top and was the first building in the country made entirely of stone. It clearly shows how advanced the ancient Egyptian culture was, both artistically and mechanically.

Another incredible monument is the Great Sphinx—a half-lion, half-man stone structure built for King Khafre. Historians have been able to learn much about the ancient Egyptian people by studying these buildings and the materials in them. Fortunately, the climate in Egypt was dry, so the writings and artifacts were well preserved.

14. **Write a subjunctive verb.** _____

15. **Write two adverbs.** _____ _____

16. **Write two passive verbs.** _____ _____

17. **Write an appositive.** _____

18. **Write two participial phrases.** _____

    _____

19. **Write a gerund phrase.** _____

20. **Write two conjunctions.** _____ _____

21. **Write two prepositional phrases.** _____

    _____

Capitalization

> **Capitalize** the first word of a sentence and of each line of poetry.
>
> > **Examples:** Jim recited a poem. The first two lines follow.
> >
> > All the animals looked up in wonder
> >
> > When they heard the roaring thunder.
>
> Capitalize the first word of a direct quotation.
>
> > **Example:** Beth said, "Let's try to memorize a poem, too."
>
> Capitalize the first, last, and all important words in the titles of books, poems, stories, and songs.
>
> > **Example:** *The Jungle Book*, "Snow Time"

Circle each letter that should be capitalized. Write the capital letter above it.

1. Anthony said, "what time does the movie start?"

2. francis Scott Key wrote "the star spangled banner."

3. edgar Allan Poe, the author of "the raven," was born in Boston.

4. paul asked, "when do you plan to visit your friend?"

5. who wrote the poems "snowbound" and "the barefoot boy"?

6. what famous American said, "give me liberty, or give me death"?

> Capitalize all **proper nouns**.
>
> > **Examples:** James T. White, Mother, Fifth Avenue, Italy, Missouri, Great Smoky Mountains, Thanksgiving, November, Statue of Liberty, *Mayflower*, British Columbia
>
> Capitalize all **proper adjectives**. A proper adjective is an adjective that is made from a proper noun.
>
> > **Examples:** the Italian language, Chinese food, French tourists

Circle each letter that should be capitalized. Write the capital letter above it.

7. Lauren, does your friend live in miami, florida, or atlanta, georgia?

8. The potomac river forms the boundary between virginia and maryland.

9. The *pinta*, the *niña*, and the *santa maria* were the ships columbus sailed.

10. The spanish explorers discovered the mississippi river before the english settlers landed at jamestown.

11. The founder of the american red cross was clara barton.

12. Glaciers are found in the rocky mountains, the andes mountains, and the alps.

Capitalize a person's title when it comes before a name.

> **Examples:** Mayor Flynn, Doctor Suarez, Governor Kuhn, Judge Brenner

Capitalize abbreviations of titles.

> **Examples:** Ms. C. Cooke, Dr. Pearsall, Gov. Milne

Circle each letter that should be capitalized. Write the capital letter above it.

13. How long have you been seeing dr. thompson?

14. Our class invited mayor thomas to speak at graduation.

15. dr. crawford w. long of Georgia is believed to be the first physician to use ether during surgery.

16. What time do you expect mr. and mrs. randall to arrive?

17. Most people believe senator dixon will win reelection.

18. It will be a close election unless gov. alden gives his support.

19. When is ms. howell scheduled to begin teaching?

Capitalize abbreviations of days and months, parts of addresses, and titles of members of the armed forces. Also capitalize all letters in the abbreviations of states.

> **Examples:** Tues.; Nov.; 201 S. Main St.; Maj. Donna C. Plunkett; Boston, MA

Circle each letter that should be capitalized. Write the capital letter above it.

20. niles school art fair

    sat., feb. 8th, 9 A.M.

    110 n. elm dr.

21. shoreville water festival

    june 23–24

    mirror lake

    shoreville, mn 55108

22. october fest

    october 28 and 29

    9 A.M.–5 P.M.

    63 maple st.

23. barbara dumont

    150 telson rd.

    markham, ontario L3R 1E5

24. captain c. j. neil

    c/o *ocean star*

    p.o. box 4455

    portsmouth, nh 03801

25. dr. charles b. stevens

    elmwood memorial hospital

    1411 first street

    tucson, az 85062

97

End Punctuation

Use a **period** at the end of a declarative sentence.

Example: Sunlight is essential for the growth of plants.

Use a **question mark** at the end of an interrogative sentence.

Example: How much sunlight does a plant need?

Use a period or question mark to end each sentence below.

1. Doesn't Sandra's family now live in Missouri ____
2. "Snow Time" is a well-known poem ____
3. Is someone knocking at the door, Beth ____
4. Didn't Janice ask us to meet her at 2:30 this afternoon ____
5. In Yellowstone Park, we saw Morning Glory Pool, Handkerchief Pool, and Old Faithful ____
6. The greatest library in ancient times was in Alexandria, Egypt ____
7. Aren't the employees' checks deposited in a different bank ____
8. Will Ms. Wilson start interviewing applicants at 10:00 A.M. ____
9. My uncle has moved to Calgary, Alberta ____
10. Corn, oats, and soybeans are grown in Iowa ____
11. Isn't Alex the chairperson of our committee ____
12. I've mowed the lawn, pulled the weeds, and raked the leaves ____
13. Did the American Revolution begin on April 19, 1775 ____
14. Is El Salvador in Central America ____

Add the correct end punctuation where needed in the paragraph below.

Did you know that experts say dogs have been around for thousands of years____ In fact, they were the first animals to be made domestic____ The ancestors of dogs were hunters ____ Wolves are related to domestic dogs____ Like wolves, dogs are social animals and prefer to travel in groups____ This is called pack behavior____ There have been many famous dogs throughout history____ Can you name any of them____ In the eleventh century, one dog, Saur, was named king of Norway____ The actual king was angry because his people had removed him from the throne, so he decided to make them subjects of the dog____ The first dog in space was a Russian dog named Laika____ Laika was aboard for the 1957 journey of *Sputnik*____ Most people have heard of Rin Tin Tin and Lassie____ These dogs became famous in movies and television____ There are several hundred breeds of dogs throughout the world____ The smallest is the Chihuahua____ A Chihuahua weighs less than two pounds____ Can you think of the largest____ A Saint Bernard or a Mastiff can weigh over 150 pounds____

Commas

Use a **comma** between words or groups of words in a series.

    Examples: Pears, peaches, plums, and figs grow in the southern states. We found seaweed in the water, on the sand, and even in our shoes.

Use a comma before a conjunction in a compound sentence.

    Example: The farmers planted many crops, and they will work long hours to harvest them.

Use a comma after an adverb clause when it begins a sentence.

    Example: After we ate dinner, we went to a movie.

Add commas where needed in the sentences below.

1. Frank Mary and Patricia are planning a surprise party for their parents.

2. It is their parents' fiftieth wedding anniversary and the children want it to be special.

3. They have invited the people their father used to work with their mother's garden club members and long-time friends of the family.

4. Even though the children are grown and living in their own homes it will be hard to make it a surprise.

5. Mr. and Mrs. Slaughter are involved with their children's lives active in the community and beloved by many.

6. If the surprise is going to work everyone will have to be sure not to say anything about their plans for that day.

7. This will be especially hard for the Knudsens but they will do their best.

8. Since every Sunday the families have dinner together the Knudsens will have to become very good actors the week of the party.

Use a comma to set off a quotation from the rest of a sentence.

    Examples: "I want to go with you," said Paul. Paul said, "I want to go with you."

Add commas before or after the quotations below.

9. "We're sorry that we have to cancel our plans" said Earl.

10. Carmen said "But we've done this every week for ten years!"

11. Jeanette said "We have to leave town."

12. Ivan asked "Can't you put it off just one day?"

13. "I'm afraid we can't" said Earl.

14. "Then we'll just start over the following week" said Carmen cheerfully.

15. Jeanette said "I bet no one else has done this."

16. "I sure hate to spoil our record" said Earl.

17. "Don't worry about it" said Ivan.

Use a comma to set off the name of a person who is being addressed.

Example: Philip, would you like to leave now?

Use a comma to separate coordinate adjectives used before a noun.

Example: Jack Russell terriers are small, energetic dogs.

Do not use a comma between coordinate adjectives if the final adjective is thought of as part of the noun, or if the second adjective carries more weight than the first.

Examples: I study in our small dining room. She was wearing a new wool cap.

Add commas where needed in the sentences below. If a sentence is correct without commas, write <u>C</u>.

18. Paul would you try to do this math problem? _____

19. They're selling an antique Western saddle. ___C___

20. It was a warm muggy Sunday morning. ___C___

21. I like Renee because she is a dependable sensitive person. _____

22. If you need my help Cynthia please call me. _____

23. Don't wait for us if we arrive late Emilio. _____

24. Vermont has green rolling valleys and lofty pine-crested mountains. _____

25. Students it's important to eat a well-balanced diet. _____

26. His calm wrinkled face told a story. _____

27. Do you have any ideas for a project Mrs. Yamaguchi? _____

Use a comma to set off words like <u>yes</u>, <u>no</u>, <u>well</u>, <u>oh</u>, <u>first</u>, <u>next</u>, and <u>finally</u> at the beginning of a sentence.

Example: Well, we'd better get going.

Use commas around parenthetical words or expressions to indicate a pause or break in thought.

Examples: We saw the fire and, yes, it was horrific. She is, in fact, a dentist.

Add commas where needed in the sentences below.

28. Okay you may have a good point.

29. Benjamin Franklin by the way also invented bifocal lenses.

30. First you need to look carefully at your sleep habits.

31. The team did after all win two championships.

32. I would like to well say a few words in my defense.

33. No that laptop model is not on sale.

34. The review of course covered material from the entire chapter.

35. Oh I would love to go to the lake this weekend.

36. Sydney volunteers at the senior center I believe.

37. Finally proofread your paper and get it ready to publish.

Name _____ Date _____

A **nonrestrictive phrase** or clause adds information that is not needed to understand the basic meaning of the sentence. It can be left out of the sentence without changing the meaning. A **restrictive** phrase or clause tells which one, and it cannot be omitted from the sentence without changing the meaning.

Use commas to set off a nonrestrictive participial phrase. Do not use commas to set off a restrictive phrase or clause.

> **Examples:** This small turtle, **crossing the street slowly,** was in danger. (nonrestrictive)
>
> All farmers **growing that strain of corn** should have a good harvest. (restrictive)

Use commas to set off a nonrestrictive dependent clause. Do not use commas to set off a restrictive dependent clause.

> **Examples:** Peggy Moore, **who grows her own vegetables,** finds gardening relaxing. (nonrestrictive)
>
> I think people **who litter** are thoughtless. (restrictive)

Write <u>N</u> if the underlined phrase or clause is nonrestrictive. Write <u>R</u> if it is restrictive. Then add commas as needed.

_____ **38.** Employees <u>who always have a ready smile</u> make the job seem easier.

_____ **39.** Any car <u>carrying more than two passengers</u> is allowed in the carpool lane.

_____ **40.** Joe <u>scratching his head in confusion</u> asked us how to get to the store.

_____ **41.** A town like Berne <u>which has a population of five thousand</u> seems ideal.

_____ **42.** The amusement rides <u>that are the most exciting</u> may be the most dangerous.

_____ **43.** Baby Alicia <u>fascinated by the colorful mobile</u> stared at it continuously.

_____ **44.** Every person <u>taking this course</u> must be a licensed veterinarian.

_____ **45.** Amy Kwan <u>who is our class president</u> plans to attend Yale University.

_____ **46.** Melvin <u>convinced of the answer</u> raised his hand.

_____ **47.** I think the birds <u>soaring overhead</u> are hawks.

_____ **48.** She is wearing the shirt <u>that she received for her birthday</u>.

_____ **49.** Uncle Ramon <u>who is my mother's brother</u> owns a software company.

_____ **50.** Aunt Ida <u>running late as usual</u> bustled into the restaurant.

_____ **51.** Each dog <u>that passes the obedience test</u> will get a reward.

_____ **52.** Anybody <u>trained in dance</u> is welcome to audition.

_____ **53.** People <u>who are overly nervous</u> may not make good drivers.

_____ **54.** Ms. Lopez <u>who teaches social studies</u> will retire next year.

_____ **55.** The smallest puppy <u>struggling to get to the food</u> kept tumbling over.

_____ **56.** The Declaration of Independence <u>adopted in 1776</u> was drafted by Thomas Jefferson.

_____ **57.** That law <u>which met real needs a century ago</u> should be updated.

Use commas to set off nonrestrictive appositives and appositive phrases.

Examples: We were watching our favorite sport, **baseball,** when you called.

Will Jason Boone, **the mayor of Springwater,** run for state congress?

A restrictive appositive contains essential information for identifying the noun that it follows. Do not use commas to set off a restrictive appositive.

Example: My cousin **Lurleen** grew up in Arkansas.

Add commas where needed in the sentences below. If a sentence is correct without commas, write <u>C</u>.

58. Dr. Perillo, a nutritionist, is an expert on proper eating. _____

59. Maine, the largest of the New England states, has a beautiful coastline. _____

60. Rubber, an elastic substance, quickly restores itself to its original size and shape. _____

61. Is it true that the poet Carl Sandburg lived in Chicago? __C__

62. The yogurt shop was out of its most popular flavor, vanilla. _____

63. William Shakespeare wrote the play *Romeo and Juliet*. __C__

64. My best friend, Nancy, has been taking fencing lessons. _____

65. Becky goes to Wittenburg College, a liberal arts university in Ohio. _____

66. Dad's boss, Mr. Tarkav, will be an umpire. _____

67. Alfred Nobel, the founder of the Nobel Prize, was a scientist. _____

Add commas where needed in the paragraphs below.

68.   Our neighbor, Patrick, has fruit trees on his property. "Patrick, what kinds of fruit do you grow?" I asked. "Well, I grow peaches, apricots, pears, and plums," he replied. "Wow! That's quite a variety," I said. Patrick's oldest son, Jonathan, helps his dad care for the trees. "Oh, it's constant work and care," Jonathan said, "but the delicious results are worth the effort." After harvesting the fruit, Jonathan's mother, Allison, cans the fruit for use throughout the year. She makes preserves, and she gives them as gifts for special occasions. Allison sells some of her preserves to Chris Simon, the owner of a local shop. People come from all over the county to buy Allison's preserves.

   Jonathan's aunt, Christina, who grows corn, tomatoes, beans, and squash in her garden, selects her best vegetables each year and enters them in the fair. She has won blue ribbons, medals, and certificates for her vegetables. Her specialty, squash-and-tomato bread, is one of the most delicious breads I have ever tasted.

Quotation Marks and Apostrophes

Use **quotation marks** to show the exact words of a speaker. Use a comma or another punctuation mark to separate the quotation from the rest of the sentence.

Examples: "Do you have a book on helicopters?" asked Tom. James said, "It's right here."

A quotation may be placed at the beginning or at the end of a sentence. It may also be divided within the sentence.

Examples: Deborah said, "There are sixty active members."
"Morton," asked Juanita, "have you read this magazine article?"

Add quotation marks and other punctuation where needed in the sentences below.

1. Dan, did you ever play football asked Tim.

2. Morris asked Why didn't you come in for an interview?

3. I have never said Laurie heard a story about a ghost.

4. Selina said Yuri thank you for the present.

5. When do we start on our trip to the mountains asked Stan.

6. Our guest said You don't know how happy I am to be in your house.

7. My sister said Kelly bought those beautiful baskets in Mexico.

8. I'm going to plant the spinach said Doris as soon as I get home.

Use an **apostrophe** in a contraction to show where a letter or letters have been taken out.

Examples: Amelia **didn't** answer the phone. **I've** found my wallet.

Use an apostrophe to form a possessive noun. Add -'s to most singular nouns. Add -' to most plural nouns. Add -'s to a few nouns that have irregular plurals.

Examples: A **child's** toy was in our yard. The **girls'** toys were in our yard. The **children's** toys were in our yard.

After each sentence below, write the word in which an apostrophe has been left out. Add the apostrophe where needed.

9. Many players uniforms are red.   _____

10. That dog played with the babys shoe.   _____

11. Julio isnt coming with us to the library.   _____

12. Its very warm for a fall day.   _____

13. The captains ship was one of the newest.   _____

14. Marcia doesnt sing as well as my sister does.   _____

15. Mens coats are sold in the new store.   _____

Hyphens, Colons, and Semicolons

Use a **hyphen** between the parts of some compound words.

Examples: poverty-stricken   sixty-three   two-thirds
                   part-time   able-bodied   brother-in-law
                   hard-boiled   short-term   red-hot

Use a hyphen to separate the syllables of a word that is carried over from one line to the next.

Example: So many things were going on at once that no one could possibly guess how the epi-sode would end.

Add hyphens where needed in the sentences below.

1. The play was going to be in an old fashioned theater.

2. The theater was so small that there were seats for only ninety two people.

3. The father in law was played by Alan Lowe.

Use a **colon** after the greeting in a business letter.

Examples: Dear Mr. Johnson: Dear Sirs:

Use a colon between the hour and the minute when writing the time.

Examples: 1:30   6:15   11:47

Use a colon to introduce a list.

Example: Our grocery list included the following items: chicken, milk, eggs, and broccoli.

Add colons where needed in the sentences below.

4. At 2 1 0 this afternoon, the meeting will start.

5. Please bring the following materials with you pencils, paper, erasers, and a notebook.

6. The meeting should be over by 4 3 0.

7. Those of you on the special committee should bring the following items cups, paper plates, forks, spoons, and napkins.

Use a **semicolon** between the clauses of a compound sentence that are closely related but not connected by a conjunction. Do not capitalize the word after a semicolon.

Example: Hummingbirds and barn swallows migrate; most sparrows live in one place all year.

In the sentences below, add semicolons where needed.

8. Colleen is a clever teacher she is also an inspiring one.

9. Her lectures are interesting they are full of information.

10. She has a college degree in history world history is her specialty.

11. She begins her classes by answering questions she ends them by asking questions.

Parentheses, Dashes, and Ellipses

A **parenthetical element** is material that is added to a sentence but is not considered of major importance. Use **parentheses ( )** to enclose parenthetical elements.

Example: My brother is in the youngest group (ages five and six) in soccer.

Add parentheses where needed in the sentences below.

1. Pablo Casals 1876–1973 played the cello and composed music.

2. The vacation site one of many choices was finally chosen.

3. The old fort it was used during the Civil War is now open to the public.

Use a **dash** to set off parenthetical elements that interrupt the flow of the sentence.

Example: Our dog—he's a mini dachshund—is too timid to be a good watchdog.

Use a dash to show an abrupt pause or break in speech or thought or an unfinished statement or question. Use ellipses to indicate a softer pause, especially in dialogue.

Examples: We're going to—you'll never guess—a tropical island.

"Well, I could . . . I honestly can't say," he hedged.

Add dashes or ellipses where needed in the sentences below.

4. The kitchen it was a dull green has been painted bright yellow.

5. You won't believe what I no, I don't want to ruin the surprise.

6. "We put up the banners don't tell me they've fallen down," she pleaded.

Use **ellipses** to show where words have been omitted from quoted material.

Example: The trees along Everett Avenue, which sloped uphill and wound gently around the park, had dropped most of their leaves in soft golden patterns on the sidewalk. (original)

The trees along Everett Avenue . . . had dropped most of their leaves in soft golden patterns . . . . (words omitted in the middle and at the end)

Read the sentence in the box. Then, follow the instructions for the items after the box.

Archaeologists already knew that ancient ruins existed near the Italian city of Pisa (famous for its leaning tower).

7. Rewrite the sentence, omitting the words the Italian city of.

_____

8. Rewrite the sentence, omitting (famous for its leaning tower).

_____

Unit 4: Capitalization, Punctuation, and Spelling
Core Skills Grammar Review

Spelling

Write ie when the sound is long e, except after c.

    Examples: chief, belief, brief, receive, ceilings

    Exceptions: either, neither, weird, seize, protein

Write ei when the sound is not long e, especially when the sound is long a.

    Examples: neighbor, weigh, reindeer, sleigh, height, foreign

    Exceptions: friend, fierce, ancient, mischief

Underline the correctly spelled word in each pair.

1. beige, biege
2. relieve, relieve
3. preists, priests
4. shield, sheild
5. deceiving, decieving
6. seize, sieze

7. concieted, conceited
8. riegn, reign
9. receipt, reciept
10. peice, piece
11. achieve, acheive
12. protein, protien

When adding the suffix –ness or –ly to a word, do not change the spelling of the word itself.
Exception: For most words ending in y, change the y to i before –ness or –ly.

    Examples: kind + ness = kindness   sincere + ly = sincerely

    friendly + ness = friendliness   happy + ly = happily

Drop the final silent e before a suffix beginning with a vowel. Exception: Keep the final silent e in words ending in –ce or –ge before a suffix beginning with a or o.

    Examples: cause + ing = causing   reverse + ible = reversible
change + able = changeable   courage + ous = courageous

Keep the final silent e before a suffix beginning with a consonant.

    Examples: hope + less = hopeless   agree + ment = agreement

    Exceptions: true + ly = truly   awe + ful = awful

Combine each word with the prefix or suffix shown in parentheses.

13. word (fore–) _____
14. active (–ity) _____
15. state (–ment) _____
16. breathe (–ing) _____
17. gentle (–er) _____
18. locate (–ion) _____

19. silly (–ness) _____
20. historic (pre–) _____
21. spell (mis–) _____
22. sure (–ly) _____
23. approve (–al) _____
24. usual (–ly) _____

Name _____ Date _____

For words ending in a consonant plus y, change the y to i before any suffix that does not begin with i.

    Examples: cry + ed = cried   lonely + est = loneliest

Keep the y if the suffix begins with an i or if the word ends in a vowel plus y.

    Examples: carry + ing = carrying   stay + ed = stayed

Combine each word with the suffix shown in parentheses.

25. employ (–er) _____

26. say (–ing) _____

27. scary (–est) _____

28. rely (–ing) _____

29. play (–er) _____

30. duty (–ful) _____

31. try (–ed) _____

32. boy (–ish) _____

33. enjoy (–ment) _____

34. obey (–ing) _____

Double the final consonant before adding –ed, –er, –est, or –ing to a one-syllable word that ends in a single vowel followed by a single consonant.

    Examples: beg + ing = begging   quiz + ed = quizzed

    sad + er = sadder   big + est = biggest

Do not double the final consonant before adding –ed, –er, –est, or –ing to a one-syllable word that ends in two vowels followed by a single consonant.

    Examples: sleep + ing = sleeping   treat + ed = treated

    cooler + er = cooler   fair + est = fairest

Combine each word with the suffix shown in parentheses.

35. slim (–est) _____

36. squeak (–ing) _____

37. slip (–ing) _____

38. beat (–ing) _____

39. chop (–ed) _____

40. step (–ing) _____

41. drip (–ed) _____

42. swim (–er) _____

43. refer (–ed) _____

44. quick (–est) _____

In the blank in each sentence, write the word that is formed by combining the word parts shown in parentheses.

45. With Sacagawea's help, Lewis and Clark _____ the Northwest. (map + ed)

46. Now that Leah is on our team, _____ has gone up. (hit + ing)

47. Leo and I can _____ make burritos for the entire class. (easy + ly)

48. Last year we visited Puerto Rico during the _____ week of the summer. (rainy + est)

49. Astronaut Sally Ride was known for her courage and _____. (steady + ness)

Unit 4 Review

Circle each letter that should be capitalized. Then add the correct end punctuation.

1. mr. j. c. moran owns a car dealership in chicago, Illinois _____

2. jesse decided to apply for a job on tuesday _____

3. wow, mr. moran actually offered him a job _____

4. jesse will start work in june _____

5. jesse is the newest employee of moran's cars and vans _____

6. didn't he get auto experience when he lived in minnesota _____

7. he also got training at dunwoody technical institute _____

8. jesse took some computer courses there taught by mr. ted woods and ms. jane hart _____

9. he also checked out two books from the library: *automobile technology* and *the automobile industry* _____

Add commas where needed in the sentences below.

10. After Jesse got the new job his family friends and neighbors gave him a party.

11. They were after all very excited for him.

12. Before the guests arrived Jesse helped clean and decorate.

13. Everyone brought food drinks and even some gifts.

14. Bob Jesse's roommate and Carmen Jesse's sister bought him a briefcase.

15. His mother who was very proud of Jesse bought him a new tie for his first day on the job.

16. Trying on the tie Jesse smiled and said "This looks good. I can't wait for my first day."

17. He was looking forward to wearing the tie and using his new sturdy attractive briefcase.

18. The guests pleased about Jesse's opportunity enjoyed the party.

19. They gathered in the kitchen in the living room and even outside on the patio to celebrate.

20. The family dog which was elderly mostly stayed out of the way of the activities.

21. "Well I'll always remember this day and I'm looking forward to starting the job" Jesse said.

Add commas and quotation marks where needed in the sentences below.

22. How did you get so lucky Jesse? asked Mike.

23. It wasn't luck answered Jesse because I studied before I applied for this job.

24. I didn't know you could study to apply for a job said Mike laughing.

25. I read an employment guide before I applied said Jesse.

26. I have never heard of an employment guide! exclaimed Mike.

27. I think I'd like to apply for a job at Moran's said Mike.

28. Jesse replied Why don't you read my guide to prepare for the interview?

Core Skills Grammar Review

Insert apostrophes, colons, hyphens, and dashes where needed in the sentences below.

29. Jesse didnt know important interview skills not at first, anyway.

30. The employment guide offered him twenty five helpful hints.

31. The guide suggested the following dress neatly, be on time, be polite, and be enthusiastic.

32. Jesse he was very serious about the job used all of the guides suggestions.

33. He prepared a resume listing these items his employers names and addresses, dates of employment, and job descriptions.

34. To become a well informed applicant, he researched employees duties and made a list of questions to ask.

35. Jesse arrived at Mr. Morans office at 345 for his 400 interview.

36. The interview lasted forty five minutes, and Jesse felt relaxed and self confident when he left.

Underline each misspelled word and spell it correctly on the line provided.

37. Two days after the interview, Jesse recieved an official job offer. _____

38. He tried to remain calm, but he was excited about the opportunity. _____

39. Jesse staid in his room just thinkking quietly for a few moments. _____

40. Then he called the freind who had refered him for the job in the first place.

_____

41. Finaly, he went to tell his parents the good news. _____

Add punctuation where needed in the letter below. Circle each letter that should be capitalized. Cross out each misspelled word and write the correct spelling above it.

73 e. river st.

chicago, il 65067

may 30, 2013

Dear mr. moran

I just wanted to thank you for offerring me the salespersons position with your company _____ you mentioned in our interview that my duties would be the following selling cars and vans checking customers credit refferences and assisting customers with thier paperwork _____ ive studied the automobile sales guide that you gave me and I feel that Im prepared to dutifuly perform my role at morans cars and vans _____ thank you again _____ I'm lookking forward to starting next monday.

sincerely,

jesse sanchez

Using What You've Learned

Add punctuation where needed in the paragraphs below. Circle each letter that should be capitalized.

1.   there is an incredible man scott targot who lives in my town   his nickname is the ironman people call him ironman targot because he has won several triathlons   do you know what a triathlon is   some people consider it the ultimate sports contest   athletes have to swim for 2.4 miles ride a bike for 112 miles and run for 26.2 miles   just one of those alone is a lot of work

scott will train from february to august in preparation for a triathlon in hawaii   scott says I wouldnt want to be doing anything else with my time   each day during training he gets up at 700 loosens up for a half hour then runs from 730 to 830   after he cools down a little he takes a 20 mile bike ride   at the end of the ride he swims for an hour and a half   yes I get tired he says but I usually feel refreshed after swimming   last he lifts light weights and takes a break to do some reading which is one of his favorite ways to unwind

a triathlon is supposed to be completed in less than 17 hours   the record is less than half that time   thats my goal says scott   hes still trying to break 14 hours and 10 minutes   scotts usually one of the top finishers

2.   sir walter scott one of the worlds greatest storytellers was born in edinburgh, scotland, on august 15, 1771   walter had an illness just before he was two years old that left him lame for the rest of his life   his parents were worried so they sent him to his grandparents farm in sandy knowe   they thought the country air would do him good

walters parents were right   he was quite healthy by the time he was six years old   he was happy, too   walter loved listening to his grandfather tell stories about scotland   the stories stirred his imagination   he began to read fairy tales travel books and history books   it was these early stories that laid the groundwork for scotts later interest in writing stories   his most famous book *ivanhoe* has been read by people around the world

Name _____ Date _____

Add punctuation where needed in the following paragraph.

3.   Cameos which are a type of decorative carving are traditionally made from hard or precious stones. Sometimes however they are made from glass imitations of such stones which are called pastes. Cameos are commonly made from gems that have layers of different colors. These gems include agate, onyx, and sardonyx for example. The figures carved into just one layer stand out against the background of the other layer. Many cameos that date from the early Sumerian period yes that's around 3100 B.C. have been found. Roman cameos were often very expertly carved with mythological subjects. Portraits of Queen Elizabeth 1533–1603 graced many English cameos.

Add punctuation where needed in the following paragraphs. Cross out each misspelled word and write the correct spelling above it.

4.   The great American pastime baseball has been around longer than many people have thought. For years, people beleived that Abner Doubleday 1819–1893 had invented baseball. However American colonists in the 1700s did they have time for games? played a version of the sport. George Herman Ruth who was better known as Babe Ruth was a great player. Early in his career he was known for one great talent pitching. During his career all twenty-two seasons of it he had a bating average of .342.

5.   The passing of time is a fascinateing experience for human beings. Marcus Aurelius Antoninus A.D. 121–180 said Time is a sort of river of passing events . . . . No sooner is a thing brought to sight than it is swept by and another takes its place, and this too will be swept away." Equaly fascinateing is the lack of uniformity with which human beings percieve the passing of time. When I asked my nieghbor Mathilda Moore born in 1928 what the passing of time was like for her as a child, she responded The first part of my childhood seemed to go on forever. Similarly, the three months of summer vacation in actuality only a quarter of a year passed by so lazyly as to seem longer than the remainning nine months. She paused, then continued, Why do you think children nowadys never percieve time as passing by lazyly? Her question encouragd me to ask my eight year old cousin about her perception of time. She said Theres so much to do every day dance class and gymnastics and playing video games that the time always goes by fast for me.

Unit 4: Capitalization, Punctuation, and Spelling
Core Skills Grammar Review

Check What You've Learned

Write H before each pair of homonyms, S before each pair of synonyms, and A before each pair of antonyms.

_____ **1.** mean, cruel   _____ **3.** terrible, wonderful

_____ **2.** bread, bred   _____ **4.** sore, soar

Write the homograph for the pair of meanings.

_____ **5.** to shake   _____ **6.** a glass container

Write P before each word with a prefix, S before each word with a suffix, and C before each compound word.

_____ **7.** thoughtful   _____ **9.** intercept   _____ **11.** undercover

_____ **8.** handlebar   _____ **10.** unconventional   _____ **12.** noticeable

Underline the word in parentheses that has the more negative connotation.

13. The concert was (unpleasant, horrible).

Underline the more precise word in parentheses.

14. The milk smells (bad, sour).   **15.** She wore a purple (beret, hat).

Circle the number of the idiom that means *undecided*.

16. up in the air   **17.** off the cuff

Underline the figurative language in each sentence.

18. That floor of the hospital is for people who are about to pass on.

19. The wrecking ball opened up a hole a mile wide in the building.

Write D before the declarative sentence, IM before the imperative sentence, E before the exclamatory sentence, and IN before the interrogative sentence.

_____ **20.** Hey, that isn't yours!   _____ **22.** I am watching the evening news.

_____ **21.** Read me the next question.   _____ **23.** Who wanted the tuna sandwich?

Write CS before the sentence that has a compound subject and CP before the sentence that has a compound predicate.

_____ **24.** Kiwis and mangoes are unusual fruits.

_____ **25.** The ocean waves pounded and sprayed the beach.

Write CS before the compound sentence. Write RO before the run-on sentence. Write F before the sentence fragment.

_____ **26.** Bart loves to swim, and he teaches children's swimming classes.

_____ **27.** Although we take the dogs to the groomer about once a month.

_____ **28.** It was over in an instant, no one saw what had happened.

Put brackets around each dependent clause and underline each independent clause. Write CX before the complex sentence and CD-CX before the compound-complex sentence.

_____ 29. The bike is broken, but Calvin will fix it when he has time.

_____ 30. Dana gave her the box of chocolates that someone had sent.

Underline the common nouns and circle the proper nouns in the sentence.

31. Before Edward could stop his car, Mr. Huang opened the door and jumped out.

Circle the appositive in the sentence. Underline the noun it identifies or explains.

32. My aunt's blog, Flying Solo, has been very successful so far.

Write past, present, or future to show the tense of each underlined verb.

33. _____ Yolanda goes shopping every Saturday.

34. _____ It will be dark before he gets here.

35. _____ Rain was predicted for the weekend.

Underline the participial phrase and circle the infinitive phrase.

36. To prepare for his audition, Zack spent hours rehearsing in front of the mirror.

Circle the number of the sentence that is in the active voice.

37. James threw the basketball through the hoop.

38. Her brother was expected on the next train.

Underline the correct verb in each sentence.

39. The colors in that painting (looks, look) lovely.

40. There (is, are) three computers available.

41. Both of the babies (sleeps, sleep) soundly during naps.

Write SP before the sentence that has a subjective pronoun, OP before the sentence that has an objective pronoun, PP before the sentence that has a possessive pronoun, and IP before the sentence that has an indefinite pronoun. Circle the pronoun in each sentence.

_____ 42. We knew the movie had already begun.

_____ 43. Stephanie and Frank spent their vacation in Montreal.

_____ 44. Sally told her to hang the clothes in the closet.

_____ 45. Someone must have seen where the dog went.

Underline the pronoun. Circle its antecedent.

46. Annette served the celebration dinner with her customary flair.

Write adjective or adverb to describe the underlined word.

47. _____ Jack is the calmest dog I have ever known.

48. _____ The group listened intently to the speech.

49. _____ The bicycle was an antique model.

50. _____ Her car had two flat tires.

Name _____ Date _____

Underline each prepositional phrase twice and circle each preposition. Underline the conjunction once.

51. Hoan pretended to be asleep when his father came into his room to wake him for breakfast.

Circle the number of the sentence that is written correctly.

52. After completing her first draft, a brisk walk helped Riley clear her head.

53. After completing her first draft, Riley took a brisk walk to clear her head.

Underline the correct word in parentheses.

54. That restaurant doesn't serve (any, no) meat or poultry.

55. The desk lamp seems (brighter, more brighter) than the overhead light.

56. Justin (can, can't) hardly run in those shoes.

Rewrite the email below. Add capital letters and punctuation where needed.

57. Dear aunt sally,

thank you again for all your support during my college application process which is now moving along smoothly_____ i would not after all have done such a good job without your patient wise guidance_____ judys input was also helpful_____

im currently working on applying for the scholarship that I mentioned to you_____ I have written an essay "aiming for the stars" to submit to the committee_____ its about my goals but it also touches on my interest in astronomy_____ the committee it consists of four professors I believe will also consider the following an aptitude test an intelligence test and an in person interview_____ ah youd better wish me luck_____ the interview is on september 14 at 315 with a ms. tara muller and it will be held on the campus of hopewell academy_____

when will you be coming to visit us next_____ if you come before the interview maybe you could help me prepare_____ some practice would raise my self confidence and also but i don't want to ask too much of you_____

i do hope to see you soon aunt sally_____ i will keep in touch with you about how everything is going in my classes at home and on the soccer field_____

Your nephew,

dennis

_____

_____

_____

_____

Underline the correctly spelled word in each pair.

58. reliable, relyable

59. couragous, courageous

60. riegn, reign

61. crankyness, crankiness

62. achieve, acheive

63. driping, dripping

Check What You've Learned Correlation Chart

Below is a list of the sections on *Check What You've Learned* and the pages on which the skills in each section are taught. If you missed any questions, turn to the pages listed and practice the skills. Then correct the problems you missed on *Check What You've Learned*.

Items	Skill	Practice Page
Unit 1 Vocabulary		
1-4	Homonyms	5
	Synonyms and Antonyms	14
5-6	Homographs	6
7-12	Compound Words	7
	Prefixes	10-11
	Suffixes	12-13
13	Connotation and Denotation	18
14-15	Word Choice	19
16-17	Idioms	20
18-19	Figurative Language	21-23
Unit 2 Sentences		
20-23	Types of Sentences	30
	Simple Subjects and Predicates	31
24-25	Compound Subjects	34
	Compound Predicates	35
	Combining Sentences	36
26-28	Compound and Complex Sentences	39-40
	Correcting Fragments	42
	Correcting Run-on Sentences	43
29-30	Independent and Dependent Clauses	37
	Compound-Complex Sentences	41
Unit 3 Grammar and Usage		
31	Common and Proper Nouns	52
32	Appositives	58
33-35	Verb Tense	60-61
36	Infinitives and Infinitive Phrases	64
	Participles and Participial Phrases	65

Items	Skill	Practice Page
37-38	Active and Passive Voice	70
39-41	Subject-Verb Agreement	72-73
42-45	Pronouns	74
	Demonstrative, Indefinite, and Intensive Pronouns	75
46	Pronouns	74
	Antecedents	76
47-50	Adjectives	80
	Demonstrative Adjectives	81
	Adverbs	83
	Adjectives and Adverbs	85
51	Prepositions	86
	Prepositional Phrases	87
	Conjunctions	90
52-53	Misplaced and Dangling Modifiers	89
54-56	Nonstandard Usage	91
Unit 4 Capitalization, Punctuation, and Spelling		
57	Capitalization	96-97
	End Punctuation	98
	Commas	99-102
	Quotation Marks and Apostrophes	103
	Hyphens, Colons, and Semicolons	104
	Parentheses, Dashes, and Ellipses	105
58-63	Spelling	106-107

Roots, Prefixes, and Suffixes

Commonly Used Roots		
Roots	**Meanings**	**Examples**
Greek		
-bibli-	book	bibliography, bibliophile
-bio-	life	biography, biologist
-chron-	time	chronology, chronic
-dem-	people	democracy, demographics
-graph-	write, writing	biography, graphic
-hydra-	water	hydrant, dehydrate
-log(ue)-, -logu-	study, word	logical, astrology
-micr-	small	microcircuit, microscopic
-phil-	like, love	philanthropy, audiophile
-phono-	sound	symphony, phonetic
-tele-	far, distant	teleport, telescope
Latin		
-aqu-	water	aquarium, aquatic
-aud-, -audit-	hear	audience, audible
-bene-	well, good	beneficial, benefit
-cent-	hundred	century, centipede
-dict-	say	dictate, dictionary
-gen-	birth, kind, origin	genetic, general
-magni-	large	magnificent, magnify
-mal-	bad	malfunction, malice
-omni-	all	omnipotent, omniscient
-ped-	foot	pedicure, pedal
-pend-, -pens-	hang, weigh	pendulum, expense
-prim-	first, early	primary, primitive
-spec-	look, see	spectator, inspect
-uni-	one	uniform, universe
-vid-, -vis-	see	video, vision

Commonly Used Prefixes

Prefixes	Meanings	Examples
Greek		
anti-	against, opposing	antiwar, anticlimax
dia-	through, across, between	diametric, diagonal
para-	beside, beyond	parallel, paralegal
syn-, sym-, syl-, sys-	together, with	synthesis, symmetric, syllable, system
Latin and French		
co-	with, together	coexist, codependent
de-	away from, off, down	debone, debug
in-, im-	in, into, within	introduce, imprison
inter-	between, among	interpersonal, intersect
non-	not	nonprofit, nonfat
post-	after, following	postnasal, postgraduate
pre-	before	prepayment, preview
re-	back, backward, again	reverse, return, recur
sub-	under, beneath	submarine, substandard
trans-	across	transplant, translate
Old English		
mis-	badly, not, wrongly	mistake, mislead
over-	above, excessive	overhead, overstate
un-	not, reverse of	uneven, unlock

Commonly Used Suffixes

Suffixes	Meanings	Examples
Greek, Latin, and French		
-able	able, likely	readable, lovable
-ance, -ancy	act, quality	admittance, constancy
-ate	to become, to cause to be	captivate, activate
-fy	to make, to cause to be	liquefy, simplify
-ible	able, likely	flexible, digestible
-ity	state, condition	reality, sincerity
-ize	to make, to cause to be	socialize, motorize
-ment	result, act of, state of being	judgment, fulfillment
-ous	characterized by	dangerous, suspicious
-tion	action, condition	rotation, election
Old English		
-dom	state, condition	stardom, freedom
-en	to cause to be	shorten, soften
-ish	like, tending to be	bookish, childish
-ness	quality, state	brightness, kindness

Irregular Verbs

Present Tense	Past Tense	Past Participle
be	was, were	been
begin	began	begun
bite	bit	bitten
blow	blew	blown
break	broke	broken
bring	brought	brought
burst	burst	burst
buy	bought	bought
catch	caught	caught
choose	chose	chosen
come	came	come
cost	cost	cost
cut	cut	cut
dive	dove, dived	dived
do	did	done
draw	drew	drawn
drink	drank	drunk
drive	drove	driven
eat	ate	eaten
fall	fell	fallen
fight	fought	fought
fly	flew	flown
freeze	froze	frozen
get	got	gotten
give	gave	given
go	went	gone
grow	grew	grown
hang	hung	hung
hear	heard	heard
hide	hid	hidden, hid
hit	hit	hit
hurt	hurt	hurt
keep	kept	kept
know	knew	known
lay	laid	laid

Present Tense	Past Tense	Past Participle
lead	led	led
leave	left	left
let	let	let
lie	lay	lain
lose	lost	lost
make	made	made
put	put	put
ride	rode	ridden
ring	rang	rung
rise	rose	risen
run	ran	run
say	said	said
see	saw	seen
set	set	set
shake	shook	shaken
shine	shone, shined	shone
shrink	shrank	shrunk
shut	shut	shut
sing	sang	sung
sink	sank	sunk
sit	sat	sat
speak	spoke	spoken
spring	sprang, sprung	sprung
steal	stole	stolen
swim	swam	swum
swing	swung	swung
take	took	taken
teach	taught	taught
tear	tore	torn
throw	threw	thrown
wake	woke, waked	woken, awakened
wear	wore	worn
weave	wove	woven
write	wrote	written

Commonly Misused Words

Below is a list of commonly misused words. These words sound the same or similar or are often confused with each other. Read through each set of words and their meanings. Then read the examples. If you are ever unsure about which word to use, consult a dictionary.

a lot
Mike hopes to make a lot of money in his new job.

accept, except
I accept your offer to work here.
I have everything I need except for the green paint.

already, all ready
I already took my weekly spelling test.
I'm all ready to go to dinner.

bare, bear
It's too cold to walk around in bare feet.
A bear sleeps in winter.

blew, blue
The wind blew gently.
The sky was clear blue.

by, buy
The plane whizzed by overhead.
Alton wants to buy a new coat for winter.

can, may
Can Shane win the pie-eating contest?
May I go to the carnival on Saturday?

cent, scent, sent
A penny is worth one cent.
The flower shop had a strong scent.
My dad sent my mom flowers.

chose, choose
Antonia chose to walk home from school.
They often choose to walk home from school.

close, clothes
Close the door, please.
Grandpa has worn the same clothes since 1977.

creak, creek
Old and worn floors sometimes creak when you walk on them.
The water in the creek flows quietly.

dear, deer
I hold my friends dear to my heart.
Deer are shy animals.

desert, dessert
The desert is dry and hot.
Rodrigo always saves room for dessert.

dew, do, due
I love the feel of morning dew on my bare feet.
Bart forgot to do his chores last night.
Homework is always due at the beginning of class.

doesn't, don't
Huang doesn't like boxing.
I don't, either.

eye, I
He poked himself in the eye.
I have perfect vision.

fewer, less
Hank has fewer baseball cards than Joseph.
Hank has less time to collect baseball cards.

fir, fur
Fir trees are evergreen trees.
Many people don't like the idea of fur coats.

for, four
I'm excited for you.
Jamie's little brother is four years old.

good, well
Have a good day.
Our team played well.

hare, hair
A hare looks like a big rabbit.
Dad is losing his hair with age.

heal, heel
That cut should heal soon.
Sammy injured the heel of his foot.

hear, here
It's hard to hear the TV when the buses go by outside.
Most of the time it's quiet in here.

hi, high
Don't forget to say hi to the coach for me.
The flag is flying high.

hole, whole

A bagel has a hole in the middle.

I always eat the whole bagel for breakfast.

hour, our

Mom takes a yoga class for an hour on
    Wednesday nights.

Our family believes that exercise is important.

its, it's

The cat licked its paws.

It's a very cute kitten.

knew, new

Kim knew all of the answers on the game show.

She bought a new dress for the occasion.

knight, night

Fairy tales often involve a knight in
    shining armor.

The stars shine brightly at night.

knot, not

Sailors know how to make and undo every kind
    of knot.

I am not very good with my hands.

knows, nose

My teacher knows a lot about the planet Mars.

Margo has freckles on her nose.

lay, lie

Lay the pillow on the bed.

Lie down and take a nap.

lead, led

It's important to make sure there isn't any lead
    in the water.

The mayor led the city parade.

loose, lose

My shoelaces came loose in gym.

I thought for sure that I would lose.

mail, male

The mail is delivered six days a week.

A male is a man.

main, Maine, mane

My main concern is that I'll miss my flight.

The state of Maine is famous for its delicious
    blueberries.

A horse has a mane of hair on its neck.

meat, meet

Vegetarians don't eat meat.

My friends and I meet every Sunday morning
    for breakfast.

oar, or, ore

Use an oar to row the boat.

We can take a speedboat or a sailboat.

Ore is a mineral that contains metal.

one, won

Liza's family has one car.

Elizabeth won the race for class president.

pain, pane

I was in pain after the book fell on my foot.

The window pane needed to be washed.

pair, pare, pear

Ted wore his new pair of cowboy boots.

To pare an apple means to peel it.

I usually eat a juicy pear for dessert.

passed, past

Roberto had already passed several gas stations.

It's best to think ahead and not dwell on
    the past.

peace, piece

Many politicians speak of working toward
    world peace.

Joy asked for a small piece of pumpkin pie.

plain, plane

Jan wore a plain dress to her wedding.

As a result of bad weather, the plane took off
    an hour late.

poor, pore, pour

I felt poor after I spent my allowance.

A pore is a tiny opening in the skin.

Would you pour the milk, please?

read, red

I read the book in just one sitting.

Damien has bright red hair.

right, write

Is this the right place to sign up for the
    karate class?

Did you write a thank-you letter to Grandpa?

road, rode, rowed

The road was dusty and rocky.

We rode horses around the corral.

Sumi rowed the boat to shore.

sea, see

Adrian has always liked the salty air by the sea.

Alma can't see very well without her glasses.

seam, seem

The seam in Melvin's shirt was unraveling.

He didn't seem to care, though.

set, sit

Latoya carefully set her tea on the glass table.

May I sit down next to you?

sew, so, sow

My mom taught me how to sew when I was just
ten years old.

Her car had a flat tire, so she was late.

A gardener must sow seeds to grow plants.

some, sum

Priya sold some of her old sweaters to earn
extra money.

The sum of 10 and 10 is 20.

son, sun

I'd like to have both a son and a daughter.

The sun finally came out from behind
the clouds.

stationary, stationery

My stationary bike doesn't go anywhere when
I pedal.

Fiona writes letters on fancy stationery.

tail, tale

The dog wagged its tail excitedly.

Javier likes to tell tales about his family.

than, then

I'm taller than you.

Let's go shopping and then go to lunch.

their, there, they're

Yvonne and her sister went to visit
their grandparents.

Juan likes to go over there because the kids
have a lot of toys.

I think they're nice people.

threw, through

The pitcher threw the ball hard and fast.

The dog jumped through hoops at the circus.

to, too, two

Dad dislikes going to the dentist.

I am too tired to cook dinner for the
family tonight.

Drake has two younger sisters.

waist, waste

Niles complains that his waist is getting too big.

Pierre doesn't like to waste too much of
his time.

wait, weight

Julio is impatient and refuses to wait for anyone.

It's hard to lose weight if you don't exercise.

wear, where

Ruthie likes to wear large hoop earrings
every day.

Do you know where the Rocky Mountains are?

which, witch

Which dress should I wear to the concert?

Zoe dressed as a witch for Halloween.

who's, whose

Who's going to take me to my swim meet?

Whose goggles are these?

wood, would

The burning wood in the fireplace
smelled good.

Would you mind turning up the heat?

your, you're

Your dad will be very upset.

You're going to get into trouble for
skipping school.

Answer Key

Page 1: Check What You Know

1. H
2. A
3. S
4. S
5. lock
6. P
7. P
8. C
9. S
10. S
11. C
12. crabby
13. sunny
14. recliner
15–16. fly off the handle
17. We've been down this road a million times.
18. The mountains opened their arms and hugged the hikers.

Words in bold should be circled.

19. IM; **Wait** until the speech is over.
20. IN; What **do** you **believe**?
21. E; Ouch! I **burned** myself!
22. D; That article really **made** me angry.
23. CP
24. CS
25. F
26. RO
27. CS
28. CX; [After I moved into town], I rented a beautiful new apartment.
29. CD-CX; Jill was right on time, and she smiled [when she arrived].

Words in bold should be circled.

30. **Ms. Chang** rounded up the group and began the tour of the **Jefferson Memorial**.
31. My favorite uncle, **Tom Fiske**, was recently elected mayor of Greenville.
32. past
33. future
34. present

Words in bold should be circled.

35. **Waiting to go on stage**, Derek started **to feel nervous**.
36–37. Phillip leaped to his feet to disagree with the speaker.
38. are
39. enjoys
40. taste

Words in bold should be circled.

41. IP; **Nobody** understands what happened.
42. OP; Ellen played the first song for **him**.
43. PP; The horse raised **its** head to look at the dog.
44. SP; **He** sent the memo to four people.
45. **Janet and Jason** met to discuss the response to their request.
46. adjective
47. adverb
48. adjective
49. adjective
50. adjective

Words in bold should be circled.

51. I don't have the time or the patience to talk **about** the complaints **of** those people.
52–53. Leaping across the stage, the dancer amazed us with her performance.
54. could
55. any
56. cutest
57. Hello, Steve,

Well, I wanted to check in with you. How was your week at the lake with Milly and the girls? We had such a good time visiting Aunt Amy. You won't believe what—no, I'll wait until I see you to tell you that story. Let's just say that her other guests, who were quite adventurous, led us into some interesting situations. We were fortunate to have mild, sunny weather most days. The drive back (just three hours on the open road with very little traffic) was even fairly pleasant.

We're so excited you're coming to visit! Even little Jason managed to say, "Uncle Steve visit," which was pretty good for a child of only twenty-two months. Wouldn't you agree? Harriet Mills, our next-door neighbor, is looking forward to meeting you, by the way.

Oh, I want to be sure I have the information correct. Please let me know as soon as possible if any of this is wrong: Flight 561, 3:10 P.M., May 22. See you then.

Amanda

58. receipt
59. usually
60. piece
61. loveliest
62. trimmer
63. cried

Unit 1
Page 5: Homonyms

1. weight
2. sail
3. browse
4. days; inn
5. floe
6. boulder
7. pier
8. loan
9. mist
10. see
11. threw; through
12. buy; beach
13. aisle
14. principal
15. meets
16. rein
17. brake
18. There
19. flew; straight
20. allowed
21. way
22. steel
23. sale
24. fair
25. made
26. dear
27. eight
28. vein or vane
29. straight
30. through
31. sore
32. board
33. sea
34. cent or scent
35. pair or pear
36. piece
37. son
38. blew

Page 6: Homographs

1. b
2. b
3. a
4. b
5. checkers
6. duck
7. can
8. alight
9. stall
10. snap
11. squash
12. quack
13. punch

Page 7: Compound Words

1–12. *Answers will vary. Possible compound words include: air-condition, airline, airport, blackberry, blackbird, doorknob, doorway, sandpaper, seabird, seaport, understand, underground, underline, undersea.*

13. water that moves quickly in a circle
14. very deep, loose, wet sand that moves rapidly
15. a snake that makes a rattling sound with its tail
16. a small circular band worn on the ear
17. a group of people who ride together in a car
18. a string or cord that secures a shoe to a foot

Page 8: Roots

1. telegraph
2. speedometer
3. hydrant
4. telescope
5. chronology
6. biology
7. cartography
8. microscope
9. hydrate
10. autograph
11. chronometer
12. biosphere
13. teleconference
14. hydroelectric
15. geography
16. centimeter
17. manage
18. aquarium
19. remote
20. primitive
21. manuscript
22. century
23. dictation
24. aquifer
25. motivate
26. spectacle
27. primary
28. manual
29. spectator
30. dictionary

Page 10: Prefixes

1. impractical; not practical
2. misbehave; behave badly
3. uneasy; not at ease
4. nonviolent; not violent
5. unusual; not usual or expected
6. un-; not expected
7. dis-; not appear or opposite of appear
8. dis-; not agree
9. mis-; spell wrong
10. pre-; see before anyone else
11. re-; to enter again
12. mis-; put in the wrong place
13. dia-; speech between people
14. de-; break away from
15. sub-; under the earth
16. anti-; working against bacteria, or germs
17. dia-; line across a circle
18. inter-; action occurring between two or more people or things
19. sub-; vessel that goes under the water
20. antithesis; opposite of the stated idea
21. hyperventilate; breathe excessively or too much
22. decelerate; bring down the speed
23. substandard; beneath acceptable levels of quality
24. interspecies; between species

Page 12: Suffixes

1. mountainous; full of mountains
2. helpful; full of help
3. snowy; full of snow
4. national; related to a nation
5. knowledgeable; inclined to have knowledge of
6. -able; able to be broken
7. -less; without end
8. -ous; full of hazards
9. -able; able to be inflated, suitable for inflating
10. -ous; full of poison
11. -able; able to be depended on
12. -ous; full of humor
13. –ment; act of saying something
14. –ize; to cause to be social
15. –ance; act of allowing in
16. –tude; state of feeling grateful
17. –ic; showing qualities of angels
18. –ance; quality of shining brightly
19. –ible; able to be seen
20. volcanic; showing the quality of a volcano
21. criticize; make a critical remark
22. audible; able to be heard
23. movement; act of moving
24. flexible; able to bend easily

Page 14: Synonyms and Antonyms

1–12. *Answers may vary. Possible answers:*
1. nice
2. plenty
3. evacuate
4. ask
5. brave
6. fake
7. well known
8. exchange
9. building
10. country
11. hard
12. empty
13–16. *Answers may vary.*
17. success
18. present
19. after
20. fast
21. none
22. far
23. hate
24. yes
25. enemy
26. never
27. dark
28. backward
29. rough
30. begin
31. build
32. remember

Page 15: Context Clues

1. someone who designs buildings
2. lime trees, orange trees, and lemon trees
3. land that can be farmed
4. newness
5. pine trees or blue spruce
6. angry
7. nervous and confused
8. fewer words and less time
9. cranky
10. Fleas, ticks
11. using words effectively
12. people who create arts and crafts
13. ill or frail
14. conveniences or luxuries
15. giving fair and equal consideration to both sides of a dispute
16. more energetic and willful than other types of dogs
17. soothed it with lotion
18. but his room was not very neat
19. but the melody can last in a person's memory for a long time

20. however, the solution remains hidden
21. Since the disease was spread easily
22. replaces the singer
23. but she was later welcomed back and praised for her courage
24. which is larger than most other kinds of pasta
25. brought many different styles
26. harsh and unpleasant
27. enemies or opponents
28. a small and modest home
29. hard to believe; doubtful
30. a doctor specializing in diseases of the heart

Page 17: Reference Materials
1. campus
2. verb
3. to carry or bring
4. gardenia
5. noun
6. out
7. definition 4
8. definition 5

Page 18: Connotation and Denotation
1. − ; +
2. + ; −
3. − ; +
4. + ; −
5. + ; +
6. + ; N
7. N; +
8. + ; −
9. N; +
10. − ; +
11. − ; N
12. − ; +

Paragraphs will vary.
Sample paragraph follows:
> Jason <u>made</u> his way through the <u>group</u> of people. He <u>walked</u> through the doorway and <u>leaned</u> against the wall. His clothes were quite <u>colorful</u>. He <u>looked</u> at everyone with <u>friendly</u> eyes. Then he <u>laughed</u> and said in a <u>pleasant</u> tone, "I'm finally here."

Page 19: Word Choice
1. thrilling
2. fantastic, picnic
3. rhythmic
4. startled, clatter
5. gulped
6. sprawling
7. dense

8. spindly, spun
9. looks like a giant bear's head
10. spacious
11. devastated
12. for hours, snowcapped
13. gaze, bone chilling
14. stroll, wildflower field, delightful
15. Jet-black

16-20. *Answers will vary. Possible answers are given.*
16. The algebra class is my most challenging one this semester.
17. The crafts store had everything from warm knitted scarves to colorful blown-glass vases.
18. Our five-hour drive across Georgia was tiring because of the bad weather.
19. The kitten looks adorable and sweet when she is snoozing.
20. The customer slowly shuffled out, murmuring indistinguishably under her breath.

Page 20: Idioms
1. J
2. C
3. A or D
4. B
5. K
6. F
7. A or D
8. H
9. E; G
10. I

Answers will vary. Possible answers include:
11. undecided
12. very happy
13. in some type of trouble
14. very strange or peculiar
15. talk seriously
16. in trouble
17. very attentive
18. was found
19. worked together

Page 21: Figurative Language
1. train eats up the miles
2. sun was smiling
3. skyscraper stood stubbornly
4. dough refused
5. sky spread its angry clouds
6. Romeo and Juliet
7. Achilles heel
8. Garden of Eden
9. "Beam me up, Scotty!"
10. Napoleon complex
11. personification
12. allusion

13. personification
14. allusion
15. personification
16. verbal irony
17. euphemism
18. verbal irony
19. euphemism
20. pun
21. euphemism
22. oxymoron
23. euphemism
24. pun
25. oxymoron
26. euphemism
27. verbal irony
28. verbal irony
29. pun
30. pun
31. oxymoron
32. verbal irony
33. pun
34. paradox
35. hyperbole
36. hyperbole
37. hyperbole
38. paradox
39. hyperbole
40. hyperbole
41. paradox
42. hyperbole
43. paradox

44–53: *Answers will vary. Possible answers are given.*
44. dirt
45. ten years
46. pebbles
47. a thousand
48. my feet are going to fall off
49. truck tires
50. a stop sign
51. a hundred feet
52. baby elephants
53. the king's entire banquet

Page 24: Word Relationships
1. cause and effect
2. item to category
3. synonyms
4. cause and effect
5. antonyms
6. item to category
7. part to whole
8. antonyms
9. accept
10. waste
11. molecule
12. courageous
13. savings

14. government
15. knowledge
16. color

Page 25: Review

1. weak, week
2. blew, blue
3. read, red
4. pain, pane
5. b
6. b
7. a
8. thankful
9. repay
10. disagree
11. foolish
12. blacken
13. thankless
14. unhappy
15. mistake·
16. A
17. S
18. S
19. S
20. A
21. A
22. S
23. A
24. A
25. great or irrational fear
26. untrue statements
27. argumentative or disagreeable
28. −
29. +
30. −
31. +
32. −
33. +
34. charming
35. comforting
36. leapt, scurried
37. vintage, convertible
38. hit the high spots; talk about the most important points
39. cut corners; do something in the least expensive way
40. pull some strings; use influence to gain something
41. hyperbole
42. verbal irony
43. personification
44. euphemism
45. reveal
46. gratitude
47. fabric
48. frigid

Page 27: Using What You've Learned

1–4. *Sentences will vary but should include the following words:*
1. knew
2. greater
3. chews
4. waste
5–6. *Sentences will vary.*
7–16. *Answers will vary. Possible answers include:*
7. misplace
8. indirect
9. useful, useless
10. measurable
11. speechless
12. tireless
13. remarkable
14. misspell
15. repay
16. refund
17–18. *Sentences will vary.*
19–20. *Sentences may vary. Possible sentences include:*
19. White clouds drifted across the morning sky.
20. The light wind was blowing leaves under the trees.
21. realistic; able to be done
22. silly or without substance
23. scared-sounding
24–29. *Answers will vary. Possible answers:*
24. skinny
25. ancient
26. rags
27. slender
28. antique
29. apparel
30–32. *Sentences will vary. Possible sentences are given.*
30. Kara's truck looks clean and shiny and runs smoothly and reliably.
31. The attic was packed to overflowing with boxes of old photographs, books, and souvenirs.
32. The terrified deer and rabbits tried to escape the wildfire.
33–35. *Sentences will vary.*
36–38. *Sentences will vary. Possible sentences are given.*
36. The sun beamed a broad smile.
37. That dog is training-challenged.
38. Oh, yeah, I just *loved* sitting through that movie.

Unit 2
Page 29: Recognizing Sentences

Items 2, 5, 7, 9, 10, 11, 12, 13, 16, 19, 20, 21, 22, 24, 28, and 29 are sentences. Each sentence should end with a period.

Page 30: Types of Sentences

1. D; .
2. IM, .
3. IN; ?
4. IM; .
5. IN; ?
6. IN; ?
7. D; . or E; !
8. IN; ?
9. IM; .
10. E; !
11. IM; .
12. IN; ?
13. IN; ?
14. D; .
15. IN; ?
16. IM; .
17. IN; ?
18. IM; .
19. IN; ?
20. E; ! or IM; .
21. D; .
22. IN; ?
23. IM; .

Page 31: Simple Subjects and Predicates

1. A sudden clap of thunder/frightened all of us.
2. The soft snow/covered the fields and roads.
3. We/drove very slowly over the narrow bridge.
4. The students/are making an aquarium.
5. Our class/read about the founder of Hull House.
6. The women/were talking in the park.
7. This album/has many folk songs.
8. We/are furnishing the sandwiches for tonight's picnic.
9. All the trees on that lawn/are giant oaks.
10. Many Americans/are working in foreign countries.
11. The manager/read the names of the contest winners.
12. Bill/brought these large melons.

13. We/opened the front door of the house.
14. The two mechanics/worked on the car for an hour.
15. Black and yellow butterflies/fluttered among the flowers.
16. The child/spoke politely.
17. We/found many beautiful shells along the shore.
18. The best part of the program/is the dance number.
19. Every ambitious person/is working hard.
20. Sheryl/swam across the lake two times.
21. Our program/will begin promptly at eight o'clock.
22. The handle of this basket/is broken.
23. The clock in the tower/strikes every hour.
24. The white farmhouse on that road/belongs to my cousin.
25. The first game of the season/will be played tomorrow.

Page 32: Complete Subjects and Predicates

1. Bees/fly.
2. Trains/whistle.
3. A talented artist/drew this cartoon.
4. The wind/blew furiously.
5. My grandmother/made this dress last year.
6. We/surely have enjoyed the holiday.
7. This letter/came to the post office box.
8. They/rent a cabin in Colorado every summer.
9. Jennifer/is reading about the pioneer days in the West.
10. Our baseball team/won the third game of the series.
11. The band/played a cheerful tune.
12. A cloudless sky/is a great help to a pilot.
13. The voice of the auctioneer/was heard throughout the hall.
14. A sudden flash of lightning/startled us.
15. The wind/howled down the chimney.
16. Their apartment/is on the sixth floor.
17. We/have studied many interesting places.
18. Each player on the team/deserves credit for the victory.

19. Forest rangers/fought the raging fire.
20. A friend/taught Robert a valuable lesson.
21. Millions of stars/make up the Milky Way.
22. Many of the children/waded in the pool.
23. Yellowstone Park/is a large national park.
24. Cold weather/is predicted for tomorrow.
25–38. *Sentences will vary.*
39–50. *Sentences will vary.*

Page 34: Compound Subjects

1. CS; Arturo and I/often work late on Friday.
2. SS; Sandy/left the person near the crowded exit.
3. CS; She and I/will mail the packages to San Francisco, California, today.
4. CS; Shanghai and New Delhi/are two cities visited by the group.
5. SS; The fire/spread rapidly to other buildings in the neighborhood.
6. CS; Luis and Lenora/helped their parents with the chores.
7. CS; Swimming, jogging, and hiking/ were our favorite sports.
8. CS; Melbourne and Sydney/are important Australian cities.
9. CS; Eric and I/had an interesting experience Saturday.
10. CS; The Red Sea and the Mediterranean Sea/are connected by the Suez Canal.
11. CS; The Republicans and the Democrats/made many speeches before the election.
12. SS; The people/waved to us from the top of the cliff.
13. CS; Liz and Jim/crated the freshly picked apples.
14. CS; Clean clothes and a neat appearance/are important in an interview.
15. CS; The kitten and the old dog/are good friends.
16. CS; David and Paul/are on their way to the swimming pool.
17. SS; Tom/combed his dog's shiny black coat.
18. CS; Redbud and dogwood trees/bloom in the spring.
19. SS; I/hummed a cheerful tune on the way to the meeting.
20. CS; Buffalo, deer, and antelope/once roamed the plains of North America.
21. CS; Gina and Hiroshi/raked the leaves.

22. CS; Brasilia and São Paulo/are two cities in Brazil.
23. SS; Hang gliding/is a popular sport in Hawaii.
24. SS; Our class/went on a field trip to the aquarium.
25. SS; The doctor/asked him to get a blood test.
26–27. *Sentences will vary.*

Page 35: Compound Predicates

1. CP; Edward/grinned and nodded.
2. SP; Plants/need air to live.
3. SP; Old silver tea kettles/were among their possessions.
4. CP; My sister/buys and sells real estate.
5. SP; Snow/covered every highway in the area.
6. CP; Mr. Sanders/designs and makes odd pieces of furniture.
7. SP; Popcorn/is one of my favorite snack foods.
8. SP; Soccer/is one of my favorite sports.
9. CP; The ducks/quickly crossed the road and found the ducklings.
10. CP; They/came early and stayed late.
11. SP; Crystal/participated in the Special Olympics this year.
12. CP; José/raked and sacked the leaves.
13. CP; Perry/built the fire and cooked supper.
14. SP; We/collected old newspapers for the recycling center.
15. SP; Doug/arrived in Toronto, Ontario, during the afternoon.
16. SP; Tony's parents/are visiting Oregon and Washington.
17. SP; The Garzas/live in that apartment building on Oak Street.
18. CP; The shingles/were picked up and delivered today.
19. CP; The audience/talked and laughed before the performance.
20. CP; Automobiles/crowd and jam that highway early in the morning.
21. SP; The apples/are rotting in the boxes.
22. CP; The leader of the group/grumbled and scolded.
23. CP; She/worked hard and waited patiently.
24. SP; Martin Luther King, Jr.,/was a great civil rights activist.
25. SP; The supervisor/has completed the work for the week.
26–27. *Sentences will vary.*

Page 36: Combining Sentences

1. Lightning and thunder are part of a thunderstorm.
2. Thunderstorms usually happen in the spring and bring heavy rains.
3. Depending on how close or far away it is, thunder sounds like a sharp crack or rumbles.
4. Lightning is very exciting to watch but can be very dangerous.
5. Lightning causes many fires and harms many people.
6. Open fields and golf courses are unsafe places to be during a thunderstorm.
7. Benjamin Franklin wanted to protect people from lightning and invented the lightning rod.
8. A lightning rod is placed on the top of a building and is connected to the ground by a cable.

Page 37: Independent and Dependent Clauses

1. Frank will be busy because he is studying.
2. I have only one hour that I can spare.
3. The project must be finished when I get back.
4. Gloria volunteered to do the typing that needs to be done.
5. The work is going too slowly for us to finish on time.
6. Before Nathan started to help, I didn't think we could finish.
7. What else should we do before we relax?
8. Since you forgot to give this page to Gloria, you can type it.
9. After she had finished typing, we completed the project.
10. We actually got it finished before the deadline arrived.
11. The people who went shopping found a great sale.
12. Tony's bike, which is a mountain bike, came from that store.
13. Juana was sad when the sale was over.
14. Marianne was excited because she wanted some new things.
15. Thomas didn't find anything since he went late.
16. The mall where we went shopping was new.
17. The people who own the stores are proud of the beautiful setting.
18. The mall, which is miles away, is serviced by the city bus.
19. We ran down the street because the bus was coming.
20. We were panting because we had run fast.

Page 38: Adjective and Adverb Clauses

The words in bold should be circled.

1. adjective; **whose** bravery won many victories
2. adjective; **who** reads the most books
3. adverb; **because** he hadn't set the alarm
4. adverb; **when** our team comes off the field
5. adjective; **that** we planned
6-9. Sentences will vary.

Page 39: Compound and Complex Sentences

1. CP
2. CP
3. CX
4. CP
5. CX
6. CP
7. CX
8. CX
9. CP
10. CP
11. CP
12. CX
13. CX
14. CX
15. CP
16. CP
17. CX
18. CX
19. CX
20. CP
21. CX
22. CP
23. CP
24. CX
25. [The streets are filled with cars], but [the sidewalks are empty].
26. [Those apples are too sour to eat], but [those pears are perfect].
27. [She studies hard], but [she saves some time to enjoy herself].
28. [They lost track of time], so [they were late].
29. [Eric had not studied], so [he failed the test].
30. [Yesterday it rained all day], but [today the sun is shining].
31. [I set the alarm to get up early], but [I could not get up].
32. [They may sing and dance until dawn], but [they will be exhausted].
33. [My friend moved to Texas], and [I will miss her].
34. [They arrived at the theater early], but [there was still a long line].
35. [Lisa took her dog to the veterinarian], but [his office was closed].
36. [The black cat leaped], but [fortunately it did not catch the bird].
37. [I found a baseball in the bushes], and [I gave it to my brother].
38. [We loaded the cart with groceries], and [we went to the checkout].
39. [The stadium was showered with lights], but [the stands were empty].
40. [The small child whimpered], and [her mother hugged her].
41. [The dark clouds rolled in], and [then it began to rain].
42. The hummingbird is the only bird that can fly backward.
43. The cat that is sitting in the window is mine.
44. The car that is parked outside is new.
45. Jack, who is a football star, is class president.
46. Bonnie, who is an artist, is also studying computer science.
47. John likes food that is cooked in the microwave.
48. The composer who wrote the music comes from Germany.
49. We missed seeing him because we were late.
50. When Jake arrives, we will tell him what happened.
51. She walked slowly because she had hurt her leg.
52. When she walked to the podium, everyone applauded.
53. If animals could talk, they might have a lot to tell.
54. Many roads that were built in our city are no longer traveled.
56. My address book, which is bright red, is gone.
57. Ann, who is from Georgia, just started working here today.
58. The crowd cheered when the player came to bat.
59. When he hit the ball, everyone stood up and yelled wildly.

Page 41: Compound-Complex Sentences

1. When Antonina came to this country, [she enjoyed her new freedom], but [she also worked very hard].
2. [Cece went to Chile during the winter break], but [her brother stayed home] because he had made plans with friends.
3. [Vegetarians, who do not eat meat, should watch their diets]; [they should eat nutritionally balanced meals].
4. Although they were both tired, [Rosa went to her soccer practice], and [Carl went to his piano lesson].
5. When Mr. Tolstoi entered the United States, [he knew only a few words of English], but [his wife was fluent in the language].
6. [The two teens had avoided injury] because they had worn their seat belts, but [the driver of the other car was not as fortunate].
7. [You should shut the gate] whenever you leave the backyard; [otherwise, the dogs may get out].
8. As we left the library, [the rain pelted down], so [we rushed back inside].
9. When we went to the science museum, [we attended a lecture on electricity]; [after the lecture, we visited some of the exhibits].
10. [The two dogs barked constantly] until the sun rose; [consequently, none of us got much sleep last night].
11. No
12. CC
13. CC
14. No

Page 42: Correcting Fragments

1. F
2. S
3. F
4. S
5. F

6–15. *Answers will vary. Possible answers are given.*

6. The two energetic boys and their little sister played in the yard for hours.
7. The sparrows flew rapidly from tree to tree.
8. As we carved the ice sculpture, our hands got colder and colder.
9. A squirrel scurried by and hid in the hollow of an old log.
10. A film crew of about twenty people arrived at the set.
11. She felt tired even though she had slept well.

12. All the students in that class are getting good grades.
13. Because the snow was getting deeper, we had to stay indoors.
14. Miguel studied two hours for the math test.

Page 43: Correcting Run-on Sentences

1–7. *Sentences will vary.*

Page 44: Varying Sentences

1–10. *Answers may vary. Possible answers are given.*

1. In many parts of the world, animals are in danger of extinction.
2. Related to the monkey, the aye-aye is a small animal.
3. Because the rainforest on its home island is being destroyed, the aye-aye is endangered.
4. To see the desman, a water-dwelling mammal, you must travel to the Pyrenees, Portugal, or the former Soviet Union.
5. By damming mountain streams, people are threatening the desman's survival.
6. Although the giant otter of South America is protected, poachers still threaten its survival.
7. Cautious, mountain lions generally stay away from humans.
8. Some Pueblos built villages in the valleys, but others settled in desert and mountain regions.
9. Women gathered berries and other foods, and men hunted game.
10. The Chickasaw caught fish using an interesting method that involved poison.
11. They threw the mild poison, which was made of walnut bark, into a lake.

Page 46: Consistent Style and Tone

1. Revisions will vary. A possible revision is given.

   The Sahara is a formidable desert. It is a barren expanse of land dotted with sunbaked oases. One of the early oases was Taghaza, also known as "the salt city." The houses and mosques of Taghaza were built of blocks of salt, and these salt-block buildings were roofed with camel skins. Although Taghaza was an unattractive village, its mines provided traders in the Mali kingdom with salt, which was a commodity that was nearly worth its weight in gold.

2. Revisions will vary. A possible revision is given.

   Well, I finally did it. I finished the volunteer training at the animal shelter. That's right! I get to start volunteering next weekend. I'm really into the idea of helping the homeless pets. I think I'll like walking the dogs best, but I totally don't mind cleaning the cages and helping in the office too. My supervisor most days will be Mr. Ramirez. He's a stand-up guy. Great with the teen volunteers especially. I'm super excited.

Page 47: Parallel Structure

1. Jordan said (that you should get there early, to get there early) and that you should eat lunch first.
2. The River Thames runs through London and (to empty into the North Sea, empties into the North Sea).
3. Amanda enjoys soccer, tennis, and (baseball, playing baseball).
4. The teacher insisted that we study hard, (good behavior in class, that we behave well in class), and that we work together effectively.
5. Juanita is as good at knitting sweaters as she is at (model airplanes, building model airplanes).

6–15. Some revisions may vary.

6. Fernando is great at playing shortstop and running the bases.
7. We wanted to see a play, eat at a Chinese restaurant, and walk around the plaza.
8. Vanessa was admired not only for her intelligence but also for her good business sense.
9. London is famous for its history, its culture, and its lively theater district.
10. Rita spends more time with her family than with her friends.
11. Houston has a busy business district, heavy traffic, and miles of suburbia.
12. The weather here in the springtime is often windy, hot, and dry.
13. I plan to play basketball, finish my homework, and do my chores.

Page 48: Review

1. IN; ?
2. E; ! or IM; .
3. X
4. D; .
5. E; !
6. The lights around the public square went out.
7. Stations are in all parts of our country.

8. We <u>drove</u> slowly across the <u>bridge</u>.

9. We <u>saw</u> an unusual <u>flower</u>.

10. Taro <u>swims</u> and <u>dives</u> quite well.

11. The <u>cake</u> and <u>bread</u> are kept in the box.

12. CX

13. CD

14. CD-CX

15. CD-CX

16–18. *The words in bold should be circled.*

16. The campers got wet **when it started raining**.

17. The candidates **that I voted for in the election** won easily.

18. **Before the board voted on the issue,** it held public hearings.

19. who are trained in weather forecasting; adjective clause

20. Before I decided on a college; adverb clause

21. that I designed; adjective clause

22–24. *Sentences will vary. Possible sentences are given.*

22. Although the exam was challenging, Mara did well on it.

23. The sales staff traveled to San Francisco frequently.

24. A huge flock of black crows has taken over the neighborhood park.

25–27. *Some revisions may vary.*

25. The recycling trucks, which usually run on Wednesday, have been rescheduled.

26. Before the city started curbside recycling, we had to go to the recycling center every week.

27. Our family has always recycled because we all believe it is the responsible thing to do.

28. The boys ate at a pizza parlor, watched the baseball game, and walked home.

29. I look up to Daniel because he is wise and ethical.

30. Tracy enjoys babysitting her sister more than cleaning the house.

Page 50: Using What You've Learned

1. D
2. E
3. A
4. D; E
5. B
6. C
7. We
8. We
9. can ride downtown together

The words in bold should be circled.

10. We put up decorations, but the streamers sagged **after we hung them**.

11. Mark knows party planning **because he has many parties**.

12. Everyone **who wants to go to the party** must bring something.

13. **If everyone brings something,** the party will be great.

14. **Unless I am wrong,** the party is tomorrow.

15. **As if everything had been done,** Jake ran out of the room.

16. The girls **who planned the party** received roses, and they were thrilled.

17–20. *Sentences will vary.*

21–26. *Sentences will vary.*

27.   In space medicine research, new types of miniature equipment for checking how the body functions have been developed. On the spacecraft, astronauts' breathing rates, heartbeats, and blood pressure are taken with miniature devices no larger than a pill. These devices detect the information and transmit it to scientists back on Earth. They allow the scientists to monitor astronauts' body responses from a long distance and over long periods of time.

28–32. *Some revisions may vary.*

28. Finally, we crawled into our sleeping bags.

29. Embarrassed by his awkwardness, Dad rarely dated as a teenager.

30. To move to the next level in that game, a player must find all the treasures.

31. Although the skies were dark and the air was breezy, we did not get any rain.

32. Curious, ferrets will explore every corner, cupboard, and drawer in the house.

Unit 3
Page 52: Common, Proper, and Collective Nouns

1. <u>Maria</u>[P] is my <u>sister</u>[C].

2. <u>Honolulu</u>[P] is the chief <u>city</u>[C] and <u>capital</u>[C] of <u>Hawaii</u>[P].

3. <u>Rainbow Natural Bridge</u>[P] is hidden away in the wild mountainous <u>part</u>[C] of southern <u>Utah</u>[P].

---

4. On <u>Saturday</u>[P] my <u>family</u>[C, Coll.] visited a nearby <u>museum</u>[C].

5. The <u>Declaration of Independence</u>[P] is often called the <u>birth certificate</u>[C] of <u>the United States</u>[P, Coll.].

6. <u>Abraham Lincoln</u>[P], <u>Edgar Allan Poe</u>[P], and <u>Frederic Chopin</u>[P] were born in the same <u>year</u>[C].

7. The <u>orchestra</u>[C, Coll.] sounded wonderful, but the <u>concert</u>[C] was long.

8. We watched a <u>flock</u>[C, Coll.] of <u>geese</u>[C] flying over the <u>Colorado River</u>[P].

9–18. *Proper nouns will vary.*

19–24. *Sentences will vary.*

Page 53: Singular and Plural Nouns

1. brushes
2. lunches
3. countries
4. benches
5. earrings
6. calves
7. pianos
8. foxes
9. daisies
10. potatoes
11. dishes
12. stores
13. booklets
14. tomatoes
15. trucks
16. chefs
17. branches
18. toddlers
19. pennies
20. potatoes
21. pieces
22. doors
23. islands
24. countries
25. houses
26. garages
27. fish or fishes
28. watches
29. elves
30. desks
31. pans
32. sheep

33. gardens
34. ponies
35. solos
36. trees
37. lights
38. churches
39. cities
40. spoonfuls
41. vacations
42. homes
43. Put the apples and oranges in the boxes.
44. Jan wrote five letters to her friends.
45. Those buildings each have four elevators.
46. Our families drove many miles to get to the lakes.
47. The tops of those cars were damaged in the storms.
48. My aunts and uncles attended the family reunion.

Page 55: Possessive Nouns

1. girl's
2. child's
3. women's
4. children's
5. John's
6. baby's
7. boys'
8. teacher's
9. Dr. Ray's
10. ladies'
11. brother's
12. soldier's
13. men's
14. aunt's
15. Ms. Jones's
16. Jim's cap
17. Kathy's wrench
18. baby's smile
19. my friend's car
20. Kim's new shoes
21. the dog's collar
22. Frank's golf clubs
23. the runners' shoes
24. our parents' friends
25. the editor's opinion
26. the children's lunches
27. Kyle's coat
28. the teacher's assignment

Page 56: Noun Phrases

1. (The guest speaker) gave (a presentation about the migration of Monarch butterflies).
2. We took (a long bike ride) yesterday.
3. (The bees) are buzzing around (the flowering bushes in their backyard).

4. (The movie that I watched last night) was not funny.
5. Lily has practiced (her gymnastics routine) over and over again.
6. Even after (the heavy rains) had stopped, (the floodwaters) remained high for days.
7. Jessie loves (any books that have fantasy creatures or monsters in them).
8. (A rowboat on a calm lake) makes (a romantic image).
9. (This salad) is tasty, but I would like (some bread to go with it), please.
10. (An old photograph of her grandparents) hung on (the living room wall).
11. (That hike) was grueling, but (the beautiful view at the top of the mountain) made it worthwhile.
12. (The car that Mr. Keller bought) should be very reliable.
13. Wildflowers grow along (this trail) in the spring.
14. (Any idea that is fresh and interesting) is worth considering.
15. (Many players on the team) have improved (their skills).
16. (Our solar system) is (only a tiny part of a vast galaxy).
17. (A look at the full moon through a telescope) can be mesmerizing.
18. Take (your heavy coat) with you on (cold nights like this one).
19. I think (that terrier mix) is (the best dog to adopt).
20. (The produce stand on Highway 45) is busy today.
21. (Books about farming) have always fascinated Malik.
22. (The apartment building on the corner) is in need of repairs.
23. For (this assignment) we will need (a computer that is fast and powerful).
24. (The players on the other team) showed (good sportsmanship) throughout (the whole game).
25. (The bats that live under that bridge) fly out (every night) and eat insects.
26. Cynthia is always looking for (a good book to read).
27. I like (movies with complex characters and inspiring messages).
28. (The chairs around that dining room table) are all falling apart.

Page 57: Noun Clauses

1. That they were angry
2. what Daniel offered for the trinket
3. who he was
4. whoever enters

5. whatever he said
6. what was making the noise
7. Whatever you decide
8. what we had planned
9. why the team has lost so many games
10. whoever owns that red bicycle
11. that we had forgotten the flour
12. that it doesn't have a carefully developed plot
13. Whoever takes us to the beach
14. whatever spots had dried on the wall
15. what we should do as our service project
16. That Coretta Scott King spoke for peace
17. Whoever wins the student council election
18. when the museum opens
19. What I like most about Harriet
20. what I read in online advice blogs
21. that everyone dreams during sleep
22. that my budget does not allow for many new clothes
23. what the referees say to the captains
24. how you made that difficult decision
25. Whether we drive or take the train

Page 58: Appositives

The words in bold should be circled.

1. **Banff**, the large Canadian national park, is my favorite place to visit.
2. The **painter** Vincent Van Gogh cut off part of his ear.
3. The **White House**, home of the president of the United States, is open to the public for tours.
4. **Uncle Marco**, my mother's brother, is an engineer.
5. **Earth**, the only inhabited planet in our solar system, is home to a diverse population of plants and animals.
6. The **scorpion**, a native of the southwestern part of North America, has a poisonous sting.
7. Emily's prize Persian **cat** Amelia won first prize at the cat show.
8. **Judge Andropov**, the presiding judge, sentenced the criminal to prison.
9. Paula's **friend** from Florida, Luisa, watched a space shuttle launch.
10–18. *Answers will vary.*

Page 59: Verbs

1. (is) scattering; scattered; (have, had, has) scattered
2. (is) expressing; expressed; (have, had, has) expressed
3. (is) painting; painted; (have, had, has) painted

4. (is) calling; called; (have, had, has) called

5. (is) cooking; cooked; (have, had, has) cooked

6. (is) observing; observed; (have, had, has) observed

7. (is) looking; looked; (have, had, has) looked

8. (is) walking; walked; (have, had, has) walked

9. (is) rambling; rambled; (have, had, has) rambled

10. (is) shouting; shouted; (have, had, has) shouted

11. (is) noticing; noticed; (have, had, has) noticed

12. (is) ordering; ordered; (have, had, has) ordered

13. (is) gazing; gazed; (have, had, has) gazed

14. (is) borrowing; borrowed; (have, had, has) borrowed

15. (is) starting; started; (have, had, has) started

16. (is) working; worked; (have, had, has) worked

Page 60: Verb Tenses

1–8: *Answers will vary.*

9. future

10. past

11. future

12. present

13. past

14. past

15. present

16. future

17. past

18. past

19. past perfect

20. past perfect

21. present perfect

22. past perfect

23. present perfect

24. present perfect

25. present perfect

26. past perfect

27. present perfect

28. present perfect

29. has

30. have

31. had

32. has

33. had

34. has

35. had

Page 62: Verb Phrases

1. were held

2. invented

3. was

4. was

5. built

6. will arrive

7. was

8. has made

9. covered

10. have ridden

11. is molding

12. spent

13. are posted

14. has found

15. is going

16. have trimmed

17. exports

18. is reading

19. helped

20. was discovered

21. was called

22. are planning

23. has howled

24. have arrived

25. have written

26. can name

27. received

28. was printed

29. are working

30. was painted

Page 63: Gerunds and Gerund Phrases

1. planting, hunting, fishing

2. Swimming

3. kayaking, canoeing

4. Writing

5. hiking

6. boating

7–26. *The words in bold should be circled.*

7. living on the farm

8. fighting forest fires

9. Landing an airplane

10. Climbing Pikes Peak

11. The **moaning** of the wind through the pines

12. The dog's **barking**

13. Keeping his temper

14. our **hanging** the picture in this room

15. laughing out loud

16. Being treasurer of this club

17. Making a speech

18. Winning this game

19. pitching horseshoes

20. Rapid **eating**

21. Playing golf

22. Planning a party

23. The **howling** of the coyotes

Page 64: Infinitives and Infinitive Phrases

1. to stand, to walk

2. to eat

3. to dance

4. to clean

5. to do

6. To dream

The words in bold should be circled.

7. to go home before dark

8. to listen to the song again

9. to serve for lunch

10. To shoot firecrackers in the city limits

11. to walk in the country

12. to use fire, **to make** tools

13. to get a new coat

14. to make the trip in four hours

15. to be on time in the morning

16. to travel in Canada during August

17. to rise early

18. to see you at the reunion

19. to enter the amusement park

20. to mail your package

21. To cook this turkey

Page 65: Participles and Participial Phrases

1. scampering

2. buried

3. dedicated

4. Ironed

5. Biting

6. loving

The words in bold should be circled.

7. showing sales figures

8. advancing across the plains

9. struck by the falling timbers

10. preparing for a career in aviation

11. enjoying every minute of the drive

12. produced in the United States

13. burdened with its load

14. thinking about her new job

15. injured in the accident

16. fanned by the high winds

17. playing the trombone

18. lifting weather instruments

19. standing near the fence

20. Carefully **looking** through the catalog

21. steadily **galloping** over the knoll

22. Cheered by the crowd

23. addressed in your paper

24. Encouraged by her boss's words

25. planning to attend the play

26. Walking hand in hand

Page 66: Absolute Phrases

1. The tree being the oldest one in the county
2. The car loaded with suitcases
3. Her bicycle having finally been repaired
4. the weather being so pleasant
5. his loyal dog keeping pace at his side
6. Bags packed
7. instruments raised proudly
8. her arms crossed in a show of defiance
9. The day being so chilly and rainy
10. The clock striking the hour of noon
11. My feet having become tingly from the cold
12. the water bubbling around the rocks
13. her new puppy straining at the leash
14. leaves crunching beneath our feet
15. The team having boarded the bus
16. her hot chocolate steaming deliciously
17. The music having finished
18. All the guests having taken their seats
19. their costumes having been changed
20. The rearview mirror having been checked
21. bushes pruned to perfection
22. The pickles having been jarred
23. Headlights beaming
24. The news story having been posted online
25. her brain working to retain all the details
26. His backpack being torn
27. its leaves having fallen almost overnight
28. his hands trembling

Page 67: Mood

1. imperative
2. indicative
3. subjunctive
4. imperative
5. interrogative
6. conditional
7. imperative
8. conditional
9. interrogative
10. conditional
11. subjunctive
12. indicative
13. subjunctive
14. interrogative
15. subjunctive
16. indicative
17. subjunctive
18. condition contrary to fact
19. necessity
20. wish

21. something that might happen
22. suggestion
23. condition contrary to fact
24. necessity
25. something that might happen
26. wish
27. be invited
28. were
29. want
30. were
31. stops
32. take
33. were
34. are

Page 69: Transitive and Intransitive Verbs

1. T; joined
2. T; wanted
3. I; exercised
4. I; walked
5. I; worked
6. T; preferred
7. T; liked
8. T; switched
9. T; took
10. T; used
11. I; swam
12. T; knew
13. T; had
14. I; splashed

The words in bold should be circled.

15. Carlos walked **Tiny** every day.
16. Tiny usually pulled **Carlos** along.
17. Carlos washed **Tiny** every other week.
18. Tiny loved **water**.
19. He splashed **Carlos** whenever he could.
20. Tiny also loved rawhide **bones**.
21. He chewed the **bones** until they were gone.
22. Carlos found **Tiny** when Tiny was just a puppy.

Page 70: Active and Passive Voice

1. A
2. P
3. A
4. P
5. P
6. The doctor told Janice to rest.
7. C—emphasizes receiver of action
8. The crowd watched the trapeze artist closely.
9. Nahele selected a bouquet of flowers.
10. C—emphasizes receiver of action

Page 71: Shifts in Voice and Mood

1–3. Some revisions may vary.

1. Jessica started playing tennis again, and she is learning some new shots.
2. The sculptor had carved a bear's head, but she was not pleased with it.
3. He fired the pot again after he applied the glaze.

4–6. Some revisions may vary.

4. If Miguel were less tired, he would go to the festival.
5. Proofread your paper, and then correct all your errors.
6. It is critical that he find the leak and fix it.

Page 72: Subject-Verb Agreement

1. P
2. S
3. P
4. P
5. S
6. P
7. S
8. P
9. S
10. P
11. risk
12. Is
13. receives
14. has
15. make
16. Do
17. are
18. pick
19. was
20. were
21. watch
22. are
23. prefers
24. have
25. are
26. come
27. were
28. borders
29. makes
30. were
31. is
32. draw
33. walk
34. is
35. enjoys
36. are
37. are
38. tastes
39. have
40. was

Page 74: Pronouns

1. you; my
2. you; me; I; them
3. you; me; our
4. I; you
5. We; him
6. me
7. We; they; us
8. She; me
9. She; you; me; her
10. We; them
11. we; our
12. He; their
13. She; my
14. They; us; them
15. she
16. he; you
17. She; us
18. I
19. your
20. me
21. you; our
22. I; you; my; you; it
23. I; him; my; we; her
24. they; us; their

Page 75: Demonstrative, Indefinite, and Intensive Pronouns

1. Those
2. That
3. these
4. This, that
5. those
6. This
7. that
8. these
9. These
10. that
11. Both
12. each
13. Several
14. some
15. Some
16. someone
17. Everyone
18. each
19. anyone
20. Everybody
21. myself
22. themselves
23. himself
24. herself
25. himself
26. themselves

Page 76: Antecedents

The words in bold should be circled.

1. **Everyone**; his or her
2. **Each**; his or her
3. **Sophia**; her
4. **I**; my
5. **members**; their
6. **women**; their
7. **Someone**; her or his
8. **each**; his or her
9. **Joanne**; her
10. **woman**; her
11. **anyone**; his or her
12. **student**; his or her
13. **I**; my
14. **woman**; her
15. **one**; his or her
16. **Joseph**; his
17. **man**; his
18. **waiters**; their
19. **student**; his or her
20. **person**; her or his
21. **man**; his
22. **woman**; her
23. **Jeff and Tom**; their
24. **Cliff**; he

Page 77: Common Problems with Pronouns

1–3. *Some revisions may vary.*

1. The article calls the mayor's plan unwise.
2. Jen was waiting for Heidi outside Heidi's house.
3. Dee writes stories, and she hopes to make writing her career.

4–5. *Some revisions may vary.*

4. They have found that hard work helps them achieve more.
5. A student should follow his or her teacher's instructions carefully.

Page 78: Relative Pronouns

The words in bold should be circled.

1. **letter**; that
2. **Karen**; who
3. **Robert Burns**; who
4. **Sylvia**; who
5. **shop**; that
6. **farmhouse**; that
7. **pearl**; that
8. **bridge**; which
9. **animal**; that
10. **regions**; that
11. **turkey**; that
12. **story**; which
13. **person**; whom
14. **hamburgers**; that

15. **Food**; that
16. **painting**; that
17. **sweater**; that
18. **one**; whom
19. **money**; that
20. **person**; who
21. **animal**; that
22. **guests**; whom
23. **file**; which
24. **artist**; whose
25. **attraction**; that
26. **writer**; whom

Page 79: Using *Who* and *Whom*

1. Who
2. Who
3. Whom
4. Who
5. Who
6. Who
7. Whom
8. Whom
9. Whom
10. Whom
11. Who
12. Whom
13. Who
14. Who
15. Whom
16. Who
17. Who
18. Whom
19. Who
20. Whom
21. Who

Page 80: Adjectives

1–5. *Answers will vary.*

6. This; old; comfortable
7. a; funny
8. This; heavy; many; dangerous
9. The; eager; odd; every
10. The; tired; thirsty
11. This; favorite
12. The; solitary; the; lonely
13. the; sixth
14. These; damp
15. French
16. those
17. A; red; the; tall
18. The; heavy
19. A; tour; the
20. The; gorgeous; Italian
21. fresh
22. mashed; baked
23. Chinese

Page 81: Demonstrative Adjectives

1. those
2. That
3. those
4. those
5. That
6. Those
7. those
8. those
9. these
10. those
11. these
12. these
13. those
14. this
15. Those
16. those
17. those
18. That
19. These
20. those
21. those
22. these
23. These
24. those
25. Those

Page 82: Comparing with Adjectives

1. more changeable
2. most faithful
3. more agreeable
4. busiest
5. longer
6. loveliest
7. freshest
8. higher
9. more enjoyable
10. most reckless
11. youngest
12. tallest
13. more difficult
14. quietest

Page 83: Adverbs

1. slowly; clearly; expressively
2. too; recklessly
3. slowly; quickly
4. too; harshly
5. here
6. everywhere
7. suddenly; quickly; around
8. too; rapidly
9. well
10. soundly
11. noisily
12. early
13. severely
14. quickly; steadily

15–24. *Answers will vary.*

Page 84: Comparing with Adverbs

1. sooner
2. soonest
3. hard
4. more
5. faster
6. most
7. fastest
8. faster
9. more seriously
10. the most frequently
11. more quickly
12. the most promptly
13. more promptly
14. the most eagerly
15. more carefully
16. hardest

Page 85: Adjectives and Adverbs

1. carefully
2. calm
3. furiously
4. patiently
5. cheerfully
6. well
7. promptly
8. respectfully
9. happy
10. legibly
11. slowly
12. happily
13. surely
14. well
15. easily
16. loudly
17. brightly
18. well
19. quickly
20. suddenly
21. cautiously
22. accurately
23. furiously
24. new
25. steadily
26. beautiful
27. courteously
28. well
29. well
30. really
31. foolishly
32. foolish
33. loudly
34. rapidly

Page 86: Prepositions

1. on
2. from; with
3. through; toward
4. between
5. for
6. about
7. into
8. to
9. across
10. against
11. over; into
12. across
13. among; of
14. beside
15. across; toward
16. behind
17. around
18. on
19. about; in
20. over; in
21. of, in
22. into
23. across
24. of; from
25. among
26. After; to
27. of; in

Page 87: Prepositional Phrases

The words in bold should be circled.

1. The airplane was flying (above the **clouds**).
2. We are moving (to **North Carolina**).
3. Sandra lives (on the second **block**).
4. An old water tower once stood (on that **hill**).
5. The car slid (on the wet **pavement**).
6. Sealing wax was invented (in the seventeenth **century**).
7. Motto rings were first used (by the **Romans**).
8. Tungsten, a metal, was discovered (in **1781**).
9. Roses originally came (from **Asia**).
10. The ball rolled (into the **street**).
11. Do you always keep the puppies (in a **pen**)?
12. The children climbed (over the **fence**).
13. She lives (in **Denver, Colorado**).
14. Columbus made three trips (to **North America**).
15. They spread the lunch (under the **shade**) (of the giant elm **tree**).
16. The treasure was found (by a scuba **diver**).
17. A squad (of **soldiers**) marched (behind the **tank**).
18. Shall I row (across the **stream**)?

19. Large airplanes fly (across the **nation**).
20. Walter looked (into the **sack**).
21. The cat ran (up the **pole**).
22. We visited the Alexander Graham Bell Museum (in **Nova Scotia**).
23. Many tourists come (to our **region**).
24. We spent last summer (in the **Adirondack Mountains**).

Page 88: Prepositional Phrases as Adjectives and Adverbs

1. They went <u>to the ranch</u>. *(adv.)*
2. The first savings bank was established <u>in France</u>. *(adv.)*
3. Fall Creek Falls <u>in Tennessee</u> is my home. *(adj.)*
4. Return all books <u>to the public library</u>. *(adv.)*
5. Mark lives <u>in an old house</u>. *(adv.)*
6. Tanya bought a sweater <u>with red trim</u>. *(adj.)*
7. The birds <u>in the zoo</u> are magnificent. *(adj.)*
8. Jade is found <u>in Burma</u>. *(adv.)*
9. I spent the remainder <u>of my money</u>. *(adj.)*
10. The magician waved a wand <u>over the hat</u>, and a rabbit appeared. *(adv.)*
11. The diameter <u>of a Sequoia tree trunk</u> can reach ten feet. *(adj.)*
12. The capital <u>of New York</u> is Albany. *(adj.)*
13. The narrowest streets are <u>near the docks</u>. *(adv.)*
14. Our family went <u>to the movie</u>. *(adv.)*
15. Roald Amundsen discovered the South Pole <u>in 1911</u>. *(adv.)*
16. The floor <u>in this room</u> is painted black. *(adj.)*
17. The dead leaves are blowing <u>across the yard</u>. *(adv.)*
18. A forest <u>of petrified wood</u> has been found. *(adj.)*
19. The mole's tunnel runs <u>across the lawn</u>. *(adv.)*

Page 89: Misplaced and Dangling Modifiers

1–4. Some revisions may vary.
1. Broken in half, the log fit into the fireplace.
2. Climbing a hill, Martin watched a radiant sunset.
3. Jolene gave her brother a bird that has white feathers.
4. Earl, examining the rosebushes, discovered many beetles.

5–8. Some revisions may vary.
5. Looking back over my shoulder, I saw the team go into a huddle.
6. To repair an appliance, you should have experience.
7. Exhausted, they still had to set up the tent.
8. When leaving the train, you will see the station on the right.

Page 90: Conjunctions

1. and
2. whereas
3. because
4. but
5. not only, but also
6. Neither, nor
7. and
8. Neither, nor
9. neither, nor
10. and
11. Either, or
12. and
13. Both, and
14. Although
15. when
16. because
17. while
18. Unless
19. although
20. Both, and
21. yet
22. Unless
23. Neither, nor
24. while
25. when
26. Either, or

Page 91: Nonstandard Usage

1. anything
2. funniest
3. wiser
4. any
5. oldest
6. was
7. ever
8. deeper
9. anyone
10. can

11–14. *Some revisions may vary.*
11. The strangest noise is coming from behind that door.
12. I don't know any of the people on this bus.
13. We have never had any problems with our car.
14. Joe needs a shorter board for the birdhouse floor.

Page 92: Review

1. adj.; n.; v.; prep.; n.
2. adj.; adj.; n.
3. adj.; n.; adv.; v.
4. n.; pron.; prep.; pron.; n.
5. n.; prep.; n.
6. adj.; v.; adj.
7. pron.; adv.; adv.; conj.
8. v.; adj.; adv.; adv.
9. adj.; n.; prep.; adj.; n.
10. adj.; adj.; adj.; adj.
11. pron.; prep.; adj.; n.; adv.; conj.
12. n.; pron.; adj.; adv.; adv.
13. benches
14. flies
15. hero's or heroes'
16. pony's
17. watch's
18–20. *The words in bold should be circled.*
18. We plan to visit **Ottawa**, <u>the capital of Canada</u>, on our vacation.
19. My older **sister** <u>Kira</u> is an engineer.
20. We ate a hearty **breakfast**, <u>pancakes and ham</u>, before going to work.
21. practice
22. result
23. is
24. make
25. are
26. is
27. play
28. proves
29. infinitive; to fish
30. gerund; Skating
31. participle; flashing
32. infinitive; to finish
33. participle; improved
34–38. *The words in bold should be circled.*
34. he, **Mark**
35. their, **workers**
36. their, **Bob and Andre**
37. her, **sister**
38. them, **donations**
39. any
40. prettiest
41. could
42. smaller

Page 94: Using What You've Learned

1. *Answers may vary. Possible answers:* which is a remote land in south-central Asia; Land of the Snows; Lhasa; who are sometimes called the hermit people; herders who roam about in the northern uplands of the country
2. which; Tibet
3. who; Tibetans
4. who; herders
5. that; things
6–8. *Answers may vary. Possible answers:* in south-central Asia; of the World; of the Snows; in the world; of Tibet; of life; in the northern uplands; of the country; to the low regions; in tents; of yak hair; about the size; of a small ox; to the nomads; in the high altitudes
9. highest
10. Some
11. *Answers may vary. Possible answers:* come; live; work
12. to sell; to buy
13. *Answers may vary. Possible answers:* or, and, because
14. were
15. *Answers may vary. Possible answers:* first, later, entirely, clearly, artistically, mechanically, Fortunately
16. *Answers may vary. Possible answers:* was done, were used, was built, was made, is called
17. *Answers may vary. Possible answers:* a system of writing based on pictures; a half-lion, half-man stone structure built for King Khafre
18. *Answers may vary. Possible answers:* buried in them, based on pictures, running up to the top, made entirely of stone, built for King Khafre
19. studying these buildings and the materials in them
20. *Answers may vary. Possible answers:* If, and, so
21. *Answers may vary. Possible answers:* of years ago, around 3100 B.C., of their writing, on pyramids, for the kings, in them, in hieroglyphics, of writing, on pictures, for a number, of reasons, with hundreds, of steps, to the top, in the country, of stone, for King Khafre, about the ancient Egyptian people, in them, in Egypt

Unit 4
Page 96: Capitalization

1. What
2. Francis; The; Star; Spangled; Banner
3. Edgar; The; Raven
4. Paul; When
5. Who; Snowbound; The; Barefoot; Boy
6. What; Give
7. Miami; Florida; Atlanta; Georgia
8. Potomac; River; Virginia; Maryland
9. *Pinta; Niña; Santa Maria;* Columbus
10. Spanish; Mississippi; River; English; Jamestown
11. American; Red; Cross; Clara; Barton
12. Rocky; Mountains; Andes; Mountains; Alps
13. Dr.; Thompson
14. Mayor; Thomas
15. Dr.; Crawford; W.; Long
16. Mr.; Mrs.; Randall
17. Senator; Dixon
18. Gov.; Alden
19. Ms.; Howell
20. Niles School Art Fair
    Sat., Feb. 8th, 9 A.M.
    110 N. Elm Dr.
21. Shoreville Water Festival
    June 23–24
    Mirror Lake
    Shoreville, MN 55108
22. October Fest
    October 28 and 29
    9 A.M.–5 P.M.
    63 Maple St.
23. Barbara Dumont
    150 Telson Rd.
    Markham, Ontario L3R 1E5
24. Captain C. J. Neil
    c/o *Ocean Star*
    P.O. Box 4455
    Portsmouth, NH 03801
25. Dr. Charles B. Stevens
    Elmwood Memorial Hospital
    1411 First Street
    Tucson, AZ 85062

Page 98: End Punctuation

1. ?
2. .
3. ?
4. ?
5. .
6. .
7. ?
8. ?
9. .
10. .
11. ?
12. .
13. ?
14. ?

Did you know that experts say dogs have been around for thousands of years? In fact, they were the first animals to be made domestic. The ancestors of dogs were hunters. Wolves are related to domestic dogs. Like wolves, dogs are social animals and prefer to travel in groups. This is called pack behavior. There have been many famous dogs throughout history. Can you name any of them? In the eleventh century, one dog, Saur, was named king of Norway. The actual king was angry because his people had removed him from the throne, so he decided to make them subjects of the dog. The first dog in space was a Russian dog named Laika. Laika was aboard for the 1957 journey of *Sputnik*. Most people have heard of Rin Tin Tin and Lassie. These dogs became famous in movies and television. There are several hundred breeds of dogs throughout the world. The smallest is the Chihuahua. A Chihuahua weighs less than two pounds. Can you think of the largest? A Saint Bernard or a Mastiff can weigh over 150 pounds.

Page 99: Commas

1. Frank, Mary, and Patricia are planning a surprise party for their parents.
2. It is their parents' fiftieth wedding anniversary, and the children want it to be special.
3. They have invited the people their father used to work with, their mother's garden club members, and long-time friends of the family.
4. Even though the children are grown and living in their own homes, it will be hard to make it a surprise.
5. Mr. and Mrs. Slaughter are involved with their children's lives, active in the community, and beloved by many.
6. If the surprise is going to work, everyone will have to be sure not to say anything about their plans for that day.
7. This will be especially hard for the Knudsens, but they will do their best.
8. Since every Sunday the families have dinner together, the Knudsens will have to become very good actors the week of the party.
9. "We're sorry that we have to cancel our plans," said Earl.
10. Carmen said, "But we've done this every week for ten years!"
11. Jeanette said, "We have to leave town."
12. Ivan asked, "Can't you put it off just one day?"
13. "I'm afraid we can't," said Earl.
14. "Then we'll just start over the following week," said Carmen cheerfully.
15. Jeanette said, "I bet no one else has done this."
16. "I sure hate to spoil our record," said Earl.
17. "Don't worry about it," said Ivan.
18. Paul, would you try to do this math problem?
19. C
20. It was a warm, muggy Sunday morning.
21. I like Renee because she is a dependable, sensitive person.
22. If you need my help, Cynthia, please call me.
23. Don't wait for us if we arrive late, Emilio.
24. Vermont has green, rolling valleys and lofty, pine-crested mountains.
25. Students, it's important to eat a well-balanced diet.
26. His calm, wrinkled face told a story.
27. Do you have any ideas for a project, Mrs. Yamaguchi?
28. Okay, you may have a good point.
29. Benjamin Franklin, by the way, also invented bifocal lenses.
30. First, you need to look carefully at your sleep habits.
31. The team did, after all, win two championships.
32. I would like to, well, say a few words in my defense.
33. No, that laptop model is not on sale.
34. The review, of course, covered material from the entire chapter.
35. Oh, I would love to go to the lake this weekend.
36. Sydney volunteers at the senior center, I believe.
37. Finally, proofread your paper and get it ready to publish.
38. R; Employees who always have a ready smile make the job seem easier.
39. R; Any car carrying more than two passengers is allowed in the carpool lane.
40. N; Joe, scratching his head in confusion, asked us how to get to the store.
41. N; A town like Berne, which has a population of five thousand, seems ideal.
42. R; The amusement rides that are the most exciting may be the most dangerous.
43. N; Baby Alicia, fascinated by the colorful mobile, stared at it continuously.
44. R; Every person taking this course must be a licensed veterinarian.
45. N; Amy Kwan, who is our class president, plans to attend Yale University.
46. N; Melvin, convinced of the answer, raised his hand.
47. R; I think the birds soaring overhead are hawks.
48. R; She is wearing the shirt that she received for her birthday.
49. N; Uncle Ramon, who is my mother's brother, owns a software company.
50. N; Aunt Ida, running late as usual, bustled into the restaurant.
51. R; Each dog that passes the obedience test will get a reward.
52. R; Anybody trained in dance is welcome to audition.
53. R; People who are overly nervous may not make good drivers.
54. N; Ms. Lopez, who teaches social studies, will retire next year.
55. N; The smallest puppy, struggling to get to the food, kept tumbling over.
56. N; The Declaration of Independence, adopted in 1776, was drafted by Thomas Jefferson.
57. N; That law, which met real needs a century ago, should be updated.
58. Dr. Perillo, a nutritionist, is an expert on proper eating.
59. Maine, the largest of the New England states, has a beautiful coastline.
60. Rubber, an elastic substance, quickly restores itself to its original size and shape.
61. C
62. The yogurt shop was out of its most popular flavor, vanilla.
63. C
64. My best friend, Nancy, has been taking fencing lessons.
65. Becky goes to Wittenburg College, a liberal arts university in Ohio.
66. Dad's boss, Mr. Tarkav, will be an umpire.
67. Alfred Nobel, the founder of the Nobel Prize, was a scientist.
68. Our neighbor, Patrick, has fruit trees on his property. "Patrick, what kinds of fruit do you grow?" I asked. "Well, I grow peaches, apricots, pears, and plums," he replied. "Wow! That's quite a variety," I said. Patrick's oldest son, Jonathan, helps his dad care for the trees. "Oh, it's constant work and care," Jonathan said, "but the delicious results are worth the effort." After harvesting the fruit, Jonathan's mother, Allison, cans the fruit for use throughout the year. She makes preserves, and she gives them as gifts for special occasions. Allison sells some of her preserves to Chris Simon, the owner of a local shop. People come from all over the county to buy Allison's preserves.

Jonathan's aunt Christina, who grows corn, tomatoes, beans, and squash in her garden, selects her best vegetables each year and enters them in the fair. She has won blue ribbons, medals, and certificates for her vegetables. Her specialty, squash-and-tomato bread, is one of the most delicious breads I have ever tasted.

Page 103: Quotation Marks and Apostrophes

1. "Dan, did you ever play football?" asked Tim.
2. Morris asked, "Why didn't you come in for an interview?"
3. "I have never," said Laurie, "heard a story about a ghost."
4. Selina said, "Yuri, thank you for the present."
5. "When do we start on our trip to the mountains?" asked Stan.
6. Our guest said, "You don't know how happy I am to be in your house."
7. My sister said, "Kelly bought those beautiful baskets in Mexico."
8. "I'm going to plant the spinach," said Doris, "as soon as I get home."
9. players'
10. baby's
11. isn't
12. It's
13. captain's
14. doesn't
15. Men's

Page 104: Hyphens, Colons, and Semicolons

1. The play was going to be in an old-fashioned theater.
2. The theater was so small that there were seats for only ninety-two people.
3. The father-in-law was played by Alan Lowe.
4. At 2:10 this afternoon, the meeting will start.
5. Please bring the following materials with you: pencils, paper, erasers, and a notebook.
6. The meeting should be over by 4:30.
7. Those of you on the special committee should bring the following items: cups, paper plates, forks, spoons, and napkins.
8. Colleen is a clever teacher; she is also an inspiring one.
9. Her lectures are interesting; they are full of information.
10. She has a college degree in history; world history is her specialty.
11. She begins her classes by answering questions; she ends them by asking questions.

Page 105: Parentheses, Dashes, and Ellipses

1. Pablo Casals (1876–1973) played the cello and composed music.
2. The vacation site (one of many choices) was finally chosen.
3. The old fort (it was used during the Civil War) is now open to the public.
4. The kitchen—it was a dull green—has been painted bright yellow.
5. You won't believe what I—no, I don't want to ruin the surprise.
6. "We put up the banners. . . don't tell me they've fallen down," she pleaded.
7. Archaeologists already knew that ancient ruins existed near . . . Pisa (famous for its leaning tower).
8. Archaeologists already knew that ancient ruins existed near the Italian city of Pisa . . . .

Page 106: Spelling

1. beige
2. relieve
3. priests
4. shield
5. deceiving
6. seize
7. conceited
8. reign
9. receipt
10. piece
11. achieve
12. protein
13. foreword
14. activity
15. statement
16. breathing
17. gentler
18. location
19. silliness
20. prehistoric
21. misspell
22. surely
23. approval
24. usually
25. employer
26. saying
27. scariest
28. relying
29. player
30. dutiful
31. tried
32. boyish
33. enjoyment
34. obeying
35. slimmest
36. squeaking
37. slipping
38. beating
39. chopped
40. stepping
41. dripped
42. swimmer
43. referred
44. quickest
45. mapped
46. hitting
47. easily
48. rainiest
49. steadiness

Page 108: Review

1. Mr. J. C. Moran owns a car dealership in Chicago, Illinois.
2. Jesse decided to apply for a job on Tuesday.
3. Wow, Mr. Moran actually offered him a job!
4. Jesse will start work in June.
5. Jesse is the newest employee of Moran's Cars and Vans.
6. Didn't he get auto experience when he lived in Minnesota?
7. He also got training at Dunwoody Technical Institute.
8. Jesse took some computer courses there taught by Mr. Ted Woods and Ms. Jane Hart.
9. He also checked out *Automobile Technology* and *The Automobile Industry*.
10. After Jesse got the new job, his family, friends, and neighbors gave him a party.
11. They were, after all, very excited for him.
12. Before the guests arrived, Jesse helped clean and decorate.
13. Everyone brought food, drinks, and even some gifts.
14. Bob, Jesse's roommate, and Carmen, Jesse's sister, bought him a briefcase.
15. His mother, who was very proud of Jesse, bought him a new tie for his first day on the job.
16. Trying on the tie, Jesse smiled and said, "This looks good. I can't wait for my first day."
17. He was looking forward to wearing the tie and using his new, sturdy, attractive briefcase.
18. The guests, pleased about Jesse's opportunity, enjoyed the party.
19. They gathered in the kitchen, in the living room, and even outside on the patio to celebrate.

20. The family dog, which was elderly, mostly stayed out of the way of the activities.

21. "Well, I'll always remember this day, and I'm looking forward to starting the job," Jesse said.

22. "How did you get so lucky, Jesse?" asked Mike.

23. "It wasn't luck," answered Jesse, "because I studied before I applied for this job."

24. "I didn't know you could study to apply for a job," said Mike, laughing.

25. "I read an employment guide before I applied," said Jesse.

26. "I have never heard of an employment guide!" exclaimed Mike.

27. "I think I'd like to apply for a job at Moran's," said Mike.

28. Jesse replied, "Why don't you read my guide to prepare for the interview?"

29. Jesse didn't know important interview skills—not at first, anyway.

30. The employment guide offered him twenty-five helpful hints.

31. The guide suggested the following: dress neatly, be on time, be polite, and be enthusiastic.

32. Jesse—he was very serious about the job—used all of the guide's suggestions.

33. He prepared a resume listing these items: his employers' names and addresses, dates of employment, and job descriptions.

34. To become a well-informed applicant, he researched employees' duties and made a list of questions to ask.

35. Jesse arrived at Mr. Moran's office at 3:45 for his 4:00 interview.

36. The interview lasted forty-five minutes, and Jesse felt relaxed and self-confident when he left.

37. recieved, received

38. tryed, tried

39. staid, stayed; thinkking, thinking

40. freind, friend; refered, referred

41. Finaly, Finally

42. 73 E. River St.
Chicago, IL 65067
May 30, 2013
Dear Mr. Moran:
    I just wanted to thank you for offering me the salesperson's position with your company. You mentioned in our interview that my duties would be the following: selling cars and vans, checking customers' credit references, and assisting customers with their paperwork. I've studied the automobile sales guide that you gave me, and I feel that I'm prepared to dutifully perform my role at Moran's Cars and Vans. Thank you again. I'm looking forward to starting next Monday.
              Sincerely,
              Jesse Sanchez

Page 110: Using What You've Learned

1.   There is an incredible man, Scott Targot, who lives in my town. His nickname is the Ironman. People call him Ironman Targot because he has won several triathlons. Do you know what a triathlon is? Some people consider it the ultimate sports contest. Athletes have to swim for 2.4 miles, ride a bike for 112 miles, and run for 26.2 miles. Just one of those alone is a lot of work.

    Scott will train from February to August in preparation for a triathlon in Hawaii. Scott says, "I wouldn't want to be doing anything else with my time." Each day during training he gets up at 7:00, loosens up for a half hour, then runs from 7:30 to 8:30. After he cools down a little, he takes a 20-mile bike ride. At the end of the ride he swims for an hour and a half. "Yes, I get tired," he says, "but I usually feel refreshed after swimming." Last, he lifts light weights and takes a break to do some reading, which is one of his favorite ways to unwind.

    A triathlon is supposed to be completed in less than 17 hours. The record is less than half that time. "That's my goal," says Scott. He's still trying to break 14 hours and 10 minutes. Scott's usually one of the top finishers.

2.   Sir Walter Scott, one of the world's greatest storytellers, was born in Edinburgh, Scotland, on August 15, 1771. Walter had an illness just before he was two years old that left him lame for the rest of his life. His parents were worried, so they sent him to his grandparents' farm in Sandy Knowe. They thought the country air would do him good.

    Walter's parents were right. He was quite healthy by the time he was six years old. He was happy, too. Walter loved listening to his grandfather tell stories about Scotland. The stories stirred his imagination. He began to read fairy tales, travel books, and history books. It was these early stories that laid the groundwork for Scott's later interest in writing stories. His most famous book, *Ivanhoe*, has been read by people around the world.

3.   Cameos, which are a type of decorative carving, are traditionally made from hard or precious stones. Sometimes, however, they are made from glass imitations of such stones, which are called pastes. Cameos are commonly made from gems that have layers of different colors. These gems include agate, onyx, and sardonyx, for example. The figures, carved into just one layer, stand out against the background of the other layer. Many cameos that date from the early Sumerian period—yes, that's around 3100 B.C.—have been found. Roman cameos were often very expertly carved with mythological subjects. Portraits of Queen Elizabeth (1533–1603) graced many English cameos.

4.   The great American pastime, baseball, has been around longer than many people have thought. For years, people believed that Abner Doubleday (1819–1893) had invented baseball. However, American colonists in the 1700s—did they have time for games?—played a version of the sport. George Herman Ruth, who was better known as Babe Ruth, was a great player. Early in his career he was known for one great talent, pitching. During his career—all twenty-two seasons of it—he had a batting average of .342.

5.   The passing of time is a fascinating experience for human beings. Marcus Aurelius Antoninus (A.D. 121–180) said, "Time is a sort of river of passing events . . . . No sooner is a thing brought to sight than it is swept by and another takes its place, and this too will be swept away." Equally fascinating is the lack of uniformity with which human beings perceive the passing of time. When I asked my neighbor Mathilda Moore, born in 1928, what the passing of time was like for her as a child, she responded, "The first part of my childhood seemed to go on forever. Similarly, the three months of summer vacation—in actuality only a quarter of a year—passed by so lazily as to seem longer than

the remaining nine months." She paused, then continued, "Why do you think children nowadays never perceive time as passing by lazily?" Her question encouraged me to ask my eight-year-old cousin about her perception of time. She said, "There's so much to do every day—dance class and gymnastics and playing video games—that the time always goes by fast for me."

Page 112: Check What You've Learned

1. S
2. H
3. A
4. H
5–6. jar
7. S
8. C
9. P
10. P, S
11. C
12. S
13. horrible
14. sour
15. beret
16–17. up in the air
18. That floor of the hospital is for people who are about to pass on.
19. The wrecking ball opened up a hole a mile wide in the building.
20. E
21. IM
22. D
23. IN
24. CS
25. CP
26. CS
27. F
28. RO
29. CD-CX; The bike is broken, but Calvin will fix it [when he has time].
30. CX; Dana gave her the box of chocolates [that someone had sent].
31. *Words in bold should be circled.*
   Before **Edward** could stop his car, **Mr. Huang** opened the door and jumped out.
32. *Words in bold should be circled.*
   My aunt's blog, **Flying Solo**, has been very successful so far.
33. present
34. future
35. past
36. *Words in bold should be circled.*
   To prepare for his audition, Zack spent hours rehearsing in front of the mirror.

37–38. James threw the basketball through the hoop.
39. look
40. are
41. sleep
42. SP; **We** knew the movie had already begun.
43. PP; Stephanie and Frank spent **their** vacation in Montreal.
44. OP; Sally told **her** to hang the clothes in the closet.
45. IP; **Someone** must have seen where the dog went.
46. *Words in bold should be circled.*
   Annette served the celebration dinner with her customary flair.
47. adjective
48. adverb
49. adjective
50. adjective
51. *Words in bold should be circled.*
   Hoan pretended to be asleep when his father came **into** his room to wake him **for** breakfast.
52–53. After completing her first draft, Riley took a brisk walk to clear her head.
54. any
55. brighter
56. can
57. Dear Aunt Sally,
   Thank you again for all your support during my college application process, which is now moving along smoothly. I would not, after all, have done such a good job without your patient, wise guidance. Judy's input was also helpful.
   I'm currently working on applying for that scholarship that I mentioned to you. I have written an essay, "Aiming for the Stars," to submit to the committee. It's about my goals, but it also touches on my interest in astronomy. The committee (it consists of four professors, I believe) will also consider the following: an aptitude test, an intelligence test, and an in-person interview. Ah . . . you'd better wish me luck! The interview is on September 14 at 3:15 with a Ms. Tara Muller, and it will be held on the campus of Hopewell Academy.
   When will you be coming to visit us next? If you come before the interview, maybe you could help me prepare. Some practice would raise my self-confidence and also—but I don't want to ask too much of you.

I do hope to see you soon, Aunt Sally. I will keep in touch with you about how everything is going in my classes, at home, and on the soccer field.
   Your nephew,
   Dennis
58. reliable
59. courageous
60. reign
61. crankiness
62. achieve
63. dripping

© Houghton Mifflin Harcourt Publishing Company